CHASING TALES

THE LOST STORIES OF CHARLES LEE

GISS 'ON BOOKS

TO ALL FRIENDS IN PENDENNACK

PUBLISHED BY GISS 'ON BOOKS
HALWINNICK COTTAGE
HALWINNICK BUTTS
LINKINHORNE
CALLINGTON
CORNWALL
PL17 7NS

charleslee@gissonbooks.co.uk

EDITED AND DESIGNED BY SIMON PARKER

COVER ILLUSTRATION: NEWLYN HARBOUR BY ALEC WALKER (CRYSÉDE)
COURTESY OF THE ROYAL INSTITUTION OF CORNWALL
AND THE ROYAL CORNWALL MUSEUM

PRINTED BY FOUR WAY PRINT LTD OF KELLY BRAY, CORNWALL

OTHER GISS 'ON TITLES

A STAR ON THE MIZZEN BY SIMON PARKER (1996 AND 2000)

SEA HEAD LINES BY TONY SHIELS (1997)

PIONEER BY SIMON PARKER AND TONY SHIELS (1999)

THE SONG OF SOLOMON (2000)

CONTENTS

ACKNOWLEDGEMENTS

Special thanks are due to the late Ken Phillipps (Tregarrick) and Pat Phillipps, without whose friendship and support this volume would not have been possible.

Many thanks also to: Dr Eric Richards (Penzance); Pat Pilkerton (Newlyn); Jan Ruhrmund (Penzance); Anne Thomas (St Austell); Glyn and Dorothy Jones (Letchworth Garden City); Jan Macfarlane (Linkinhorne); Phyl Hellyar (Truro); Donald Rawe (Chapel Amble); Douglas Williams (Newlyn); John E White (University of North Carolina); Jon Massey (Plymouth); Marjorie Bird (St Mawgan); Diana Ball (St Mawgan); Derek Williams (Oswestry); Phyllis Dennison (Letchworth Garden City); Ken and Mavis Parker (Newlyn); Cyril Hart (Coverack); Roger Langley (Sussex); Hubert Eplett (Trevarrian); Phyllis Marshall (Letchworth Garden City); Mrs B M Andrews (Penzance); Ronald Jennings (Letchworth Garden City); Kenneth Johnson (Letchworth Garden City); Dr James Whetter (Gorran); Peter Lee (Southampton); Harry Woodhouse (St Austell); Fred Johns (Portloe); John Curnow Laity (Penzance); George Bedner (Exeter); Ivan and Heather Corbett (Mount Hawke); Chris Williams (Newlyn); Charles Causley (Launceston)

FOREWORD

F OR ANYONE born and brought up in Cornwall the
worst thing that can happen in life is to be obliged to
spend a long period away from their home town or
village. I have been obliged to suffer this misery on two
occasions and I was often reduced to depression, longing
for a sight of Mount's Bay and the sound of Cornish
dialect.

Fortunately on both occasions I had a copy of *Cornish
Tales* by Charles Lee (J M Dent & Sons 1941) always by
me. It contained *The Widow Woman* and from each bout of
melancholy I was saved from utter dejection by reading this
small masterpiece. From the first paragraph I was immediately at home, whatever my immediate surroundings, be
they the sights, sounds and smells of the Far East, or the
grim environment and atmosphere of Paddington.
Pendennack folk, Mis' Pollard, Uncle Billy Jenkin, John
Trelill, Mary Poljew and, of course, Clunker, not to mention the innate sense of the atmosphere of a small Cornish
fishing village, so beautifully evoked, carried me to
Newlyn.

I completely wore out my first copy but was lucky
enough to find a second. I am now on my third! *Cornish
Tales* also contains a number of short stories, all very good,
and Lee's mastery of the local dialect is superb.

Subsequently I have read Lee's other novels, *Paul Carah Cornishman, Cynthia In The West* and *Dorinda's Birthday,* his short stories and his description of *The Vale of Lanherne.* All are excellent but *The Widow Woman* is, for me, the treasure.

Simon Parker is the undoubted expert on Charles Lee and he has nobly persevered for many years tracing Lee's obscure, lesser known works, and details of his life. It was no easy task and his enquiries have even involved contact with the USA to consult the Dent archives there. His friendship with the late Kenneth C Phillipps also acted as a great encouragement.

Simon has now produced for us the first biography of Charles Lee in the form of an extended introduction to this volume. In addition, as a result of his careful and patient work of countless hours over many years, we are now able to read for the first time a number of Lee's hitherto "lost" writings. I feel that he is to be highly commended for his labours which have been a work of love and I am honoured to have been invited to provide a foreword.

— DR ERIC RICHARDS
PENZANCE 2002

CHARLES LEE – A LIFE

THE NOVELIST Charles Lee loved his adopted land and gave Cornwall something to be proud of – a body of work reflecting the ways of ordinary people in that twilight period between the "old days" and "modern times".

He deserves to be hailed a hero in Cornwall, akin in stature and revered in the manner of Dylan Thomas in Wales, Thomas Hardy in England, Robert Burns in Scotland, and Sean O'Casey in Ireland. Yet Lee scarcely achieves a mention in most books on the literary figures of Cornwall.

The author of five novels – *The Widow Woman, Our Little Town, Paul Carah Cornishman, Dorinda's Birthday* and *Cynthia In The West,* plus a string of short stories and plays – Lee was undoubtedly an enigma, who wrote almost exclusively about Cornwall. And it was as if, without the inspiration of the people and places he came to love so deeply, his power of creativity was extinguished.

To begin to understand this multi-talented individual it is necessary to look to his family background.

Charles James Lee was born on 2nd March 1870 at Seaton House, Stockwell Green, London. His father was James Noah Lee, an artist; his mother, Elizabeth, née Read. He had two sisters, Winnie and Lily, and two brothers,

Edward and Leonard. So convinced was James Noah of his son's talents that he secretly submitted a poem by the then 18-year-old Charles to the *Leisure Hour* magazine. Subsequently the same magazine serialised *The Widow Woman* in 1896.

The Lees were an extremely theatrical family, who would put on plays and shows to entertain relatives and friends. His sister Winnie was an accomplished painter whose watercolours of flowers were said to have displayed a rare gift. Sadly, Winnie suffered from acute depression and eventually destroyed all her work before taking her own life by stepping in front of a bus. Lily, who was also known to younger family members as Auntie Billy or Alice, was a dramatic character who would wander about the house and garden quoting long chunks of Shakespeare.

Charles' grandfather, Norman E Lee, was a painter, who specialised in watercolours and etchings. He led the Artists' Benevolent Fund, was a friend of Heath Robinson and Wyndham Lewis, and knew Lord Tennyson and Ford Madox Ford.

So, surrounded by creative souls, it was inevitable that the young Charles would develop a talent in some area of the arts. In fact his gift spanned literature, drama and music. He received a BA Honours from London University in 1889 and went on to develop as an intellectual, author, playwright, satirist, poet, editor and pianist.

But what of the man himself? What factors led him to pen some of the most sensitive tales ever written in Cornwall?

Lee was a true romantic, both in his personal life and in the way in which he viewed the world. He loved all living things, and especially birds.

Lee loved and, one might even say, worshiped Nature to such an extent that it is impossible to read his stories without being totally immersed in the Cornish countryside. He wrote of the flora and fauna of Cornwall not only with an artist's eloquence, but with honesty, warmth and a deep knowledge.

In the descriptive passages in the novels themselves, his own journals and notes, he makes many references to the natural world and particularly to birds, trees and flowers. There are even several entries in his journals where he made musical notations of bird song.

And in *The Vale of Lanherne*, a guide book to St Mawgan in Pydar written by Lee during his time there but only published in 1984 (Dyllansow Truran, edited by Phyl Hellyar), he makes many references to the parish's natural beauties, as illustrated in this irresistible passage: "One likes to think that the glamour of the Celtic woodlands was not altogether dissipated from the chimneys of mine and cottage, but lay dormant, till the new roots struck down and drew it out again. At any rate, from whatever reason, whether of soil or climate or situation, our Cornish woods have a charm, an out-of-the-way beauty of their own. Nowhere do rooted creatures display a more wayward grace, a bolder eccentricity. They are especially wonderful in early spring before a leaf appears, when the elms are twigged with red coral, the ash-trees nibbed with black coral, the oaks with their horizontal branches overgrown with moss and fern, the larches covered with livid efflorescence of blue-grey lichen, the dull sheen of the ivy that wreaths the trees and carpets the ground, and the amazingly bright glitter of the holly leaves, make up an unearthly vegetation, such as might wave in a league-deep sea."

Charles Lee visited Cornwall initially because of ill health and for a period of "nervous recuperation". But he soon came to love the people and places to such an extent that he settled for several years. His portraits of Cornwall are as enjoyable today as they were in 1900 – and perhaps more relevant – and he will remain one of the finest story-tellers of his, or any other, age. His characters possess a unique Cornish voice and outlook.

Sadly for his later readers, he left Cornwall for good in 1907, the only physical commemoration of his stay being a tablet in the belfry of St Mawgan church stating that Lee was organist there from 1900 to 1905. The tablet was erect-ed by his widow, Olive, and reads: "To the Glory of God and in Loving Memory of Charles Lee, author of *Cornish Tales*. Organist in this church 1900-1905. This tablet was placed here by his widow on the occasion of the re-dedica-tion of the bells 9th August 1958."

Lee was tempted away from the land he had grown to love by the idealistic and artistic community which was developing at Letchworth Garden City in Hertfordshire. He moved into 113 Wilbury Road, one of a number of exhibition houses being built at the time to showcase the visionary new architecture, and named the property

Lanvean, reflecting his deep affection for Cornwall. For many years Lee was the highly respected senior editor for the publisher, J M Dent. He was known as "the man with the green pen" by both his employers and by grateful authors whose work he tidied and polished. He spent much of his spare time composing pantomime scores and teaching piano to the young women of Letchworth.

Lee's first marriage, to Emmie, a woman devoted to the theatre and literature, has been said by some to have been unhappy, though there is no firm evidence of this. Olive, by contrast, who was many years his junior and whom he married following Emmie's death, shared his romanticism. He loved her greatly and it is clear from his letters to her that they were in love even before Emmie died, the couple indulging in clandestine meetings in the jungle of a nearby common.

Olive, like Charles, came from an artistic family and they met when she became his piano pupil. He was said to have been a gifted teacher, with several elderly Letchworth ladies still fondly recalling their lessons with him.

Life with the Lees, it seems, was nothing short of idyllic. Charles and Olive were an ideally suited couple despite the difference in their ages.

Charles was very softly spoken, and in later years rarely said anything at all from one day to the next. The only communication on some days might be "hello" or "goodnight" in a slow, gentle little voice to his wife, whom he addressed as "O" or "Pussy". There was never any talk of children, and little interest was paid to other people's offspring. Charles would hardly even acknowledge the presence of a child in the house, but if a relative was visiting he would quietly reach over and take a sweet from a bowl and place it into the child's hand without a word.

He was completely impractical, unable even to feed the cats, to which Olive was devoted. Olive, who was almost as impractical, cared little for her surroundings, preferring to devote her time to the enjoyment of the arts and nature. Such was her lack of domesticity, that if she left Charles some lunch on the stove while she went out, it would consist of a pan of water in which was placed an unskinned onion with the whiskers still attached.

Olive was girlish, dizzy even, having no regard for the fine furniture and "things", as she described the ornaments; she would spill hot tea on the Chippendale without a thought. Such objects were of no consequence, her mind being on greater and higher things – love, nature, music, and especially the work of Benjamin Britten. She was a will o' the wisp and would fly along on her bicycle, a huge hat tied under her chin, her voluminous dress flying, shouting: "I'm as free as a bird."

Both Charles and Olive were consumed by the new idealism sweeping the intellectual classes. They were vegetarian and socialist. In later years, Charles was a firm agnostic and possibly an atheist, while Olive went further and would throw up her hands in disbelief at the very idea of there being a god.

Their god was nature itself, a theme expressed over and over again in virtually everything he wrote. Take this extract from *St Cridda*, in which Lee espouses environmental views which continue to be echoed today:

"So they rested, awaiting a sign. For in those days Nature was still the kindly mother, sedulously watching over the affairs of men, interposing at every turn to warn and direct them, showing her face to questioners in the sky, writing messages in flowers along the hedgerows, and speaking to them in the voices of birds and beasts. Now she is old, a feeble grandame mumbling in the chimney corner, no one regarding what she says."

It is clear from such passages that Lee was striving to be something more than a simple storyteller. He was concerned with many fundamental truths, and while not being at all religious in the conventional sense, despite being organist at St Mawgan Church for almost five years, many of his tales, particularly the prologues to his short stories, read like sermons on the way in which he believed life ought to be lived.

While not following an orthodox creed, he was nevertheless a deeply spiritual man, and these "Gospels According to Charles Lee" often take the form of a discourse on what he regarded as the Church's sometimes hypocritical attitude to Nature.

This is graphically illustrated in *Langarrock Great Tree*, a beautifully eloquent story which would likely fire the resolve of any 21st Century eco-warrior. Lee concludes his tale, following the final indignity suffered by the mighty beech at the hands of none other that the zealous young rector himself, by writing: "So fell Langarrock Great Tree, a martyr, as I will always maintain, to religious intolerance. The Rector, to be sure, laughs when I tell him so; and I will do him the justice to say that he seems quite unconscious of the inheritance of obscure rancour which was the real motive that urged him to the deed."

And as if to stress the point still further, a character in *The Heroic Exploits of the Five Johns* is openly belligerent about the church.

"I haven' been drunk, not since Band of Hope meeting last Christmas," said John, moistening his lips. "I always get drunk then," he explained, "to show I an't one of 'em."

Incidentally, the line "drinking to show I ent one of 'un" can be found in one of Lee's journals, the slight changes in spelling and structure indicating his careful study of dialect and the development of his understanding of the idiom.

This theme of religious intolerance is repeated again and again throughout Lee's work and seems quite central to his thinking. He was by no means opposed to the Church per se, and possibly even hankered after the elusive security of a firm faith. But he felt the religious establishment not only failed the poor and the faithful, but actually worked against the good of the people.

Yes, they are tales, and many might dismiss them as merely that, but they are also parables, *St Lidgy and the Giant* and *Wisht Wood* being particularly compelling examples. Does Lee really mean us to interpret the piskies in *Wisht Wood* literally, as small people? I prefer to think so. But those of a less romantic leaning than Lee or myself might prefer to interpret them as symbolising our lost traditions; in the same way as these small people, red caps, call them what you will, diminish in stature without the nourishment of acknowledgement, so our old ways and customs fade and disappear if they are not regularly observed.

This also begs the question as to whether J M Barrie, when penning Tinkerbell's immortal words ("Every time a child says 'I don't believe in fairies' there is a little fairy somewhere that falls down dead" – *Peter Pan* 1928), had come across Lee's account of the Pobyl Vean, or small folk ("The people love us, for the sake of the old times; but now that they begin to think new thoughts, they are in danger of forgetting us; and forgotten, we perish" – *Wisht Wood* 1911).

In the following passage from *Wisht Wood*, the "great Preacher" must surely be none other than John Wesley himself, who was naturally no great enthusiast for the ancient pagan or Celtic traditions of Cornwall.

"Others again declare the piskies to be the ancient pagan gods of Cornwall; and this to me is the most probable theory. Being gods, they subsist on worship and belief; without these they perish. Tiny as they are now, in the old days they were tall and stout, far exceeding mankind in stature. You have heard of the Cornish giants, well these were they. But on the day when the first millstone with its saintly cargo kissed the pebbles under Cape Cornwall, they began to shrink and shrivel. As the years passed and the old beliefs faded, they dwindled, until at the time of my story, the time when the great preacher came across the Tamar, they were no bigger than children's dolls. That was before the folk of west Cornwall were so foolish as to make roads, which only serve to let in tourists and other undesirable persons..."

Likewise, he writes in *St Lidgy and the Giant*: "In those days merriment was permitted to the saints, and a sour face was not considered essential to holiness; rather it was considered a badge of obscure sin."

Perhaps Lee's true beliefs can be found in the words of St Lidgy himself, who chose a simpler faith, "solemnly renounced his wisdom and refrained thenceforth from all speculations, questionings, ponderings and profundities, perceiving them in their true light as superfluous baggage, weighty hindrances to the upward flight of the soul. Watching the birds one day, he made a parable, thus: 'As for the gulls and ravens, so for the spirit of man. It needs but two wings to carry it to heaven; and the name of the right wing is God is Good, and of the left, Praise God. To these will I trust'."

———————◆○◆———————

One person who knew Lee well was Phyl Hellyar of Truro, the person responsible for publishing *The Vale of Lanherne*. She said of him: "He was a remarkable man of his time; rather a square peg in a round hole. A very gentle and modest-natured man, his family and his fellow workers considered him a walking encyclopaedia. He was artistic to his finger tips and an excellent pianist and composer, always more comfortable with his books and piano than with people. In his later years he became almost a recluse but remained a very gentle, likeable old man, full of knowledge."

But there was undoubtedly also a melancholia to this sensitive old man, who had unaccountably abandoned his gift of creativity.

Some 34 years before his death, on 12th October 1922, Lee wrote to his employer at Dent's, E F Bozman, a kindly man who thought very highly of his talented employee. It was an intriguing letter and may yet hold the secret of his enigmatic life. It was a full decade after the appearance of *Dorinda's Birthday*, Lee's poorly received final masterpiece, and Lee was replying to a letter in which Bozman had enquired about his contentment, saying: "I hope you are happy. I only wish with all my heart that you could be doing what I believe you were really meant for – a litterateur of really valuable quality."

Lee's reply read: "I thank you most cordially for your kind inquiries. Do you know Swift's motto 'Much health, little wealth, and a life by stealth'? The first item has never come my way, the second and third are easy of attainment, thank goodness. The work I am doing gives me the opportunity of securing them, and is not without its agreeable moments, especially when I can bring some special knowledge to bear on it and can feel that I am thereby justifying my connection with J M Dent & Co."

Lee then ended the letter with the curious line: "There was somebody, long ago, who wrote little stories of country folk, but it wasn't me."

Those few words, buried for years in the vaults of the

University of North Carolina (which acquired the entire Dent archive) perhaps go some way to explaining why a writer of such indisputable talent did not go on to become a leading literary figure of the 20th Century. Alas, though he lived to the age of 86, he hardly wrote another line of original material.

But this lack of recognition would likely be of little consequence to Lee, who might simply answer: "At this the gentle reader may grieve: surely without reason, unless he believes that his fame on earth is a matter of consequence or solicitude to the happy dead."

Charles James Lee died on 11th May 1956, aged 86. He was cremated at Golders Green and his ashes scattered by his housekeeper Glyn Jones under a dome-shaped cherry tree, from which he and Olive were said to have derived much pleasure and under which they would lie in a hammock. On his death certificate, under the column headed "Occupation" is written "Author".

Olive died on December 28, 1967 in a nursing home at Royston. She had earlier been admitted to Hitchin Hospital and then transferred to an asylum, where she was put in a strait jacket, until rescued by Glyn Jones. Her ashes were scattered at Radwell Lane, where she liked to feed the swans.

In conclusion, it seems only right to leave the final lines of this introduction to Lee himself, expressing, as he so often did, his great love of Cornwall and her people.

"Dear Cornish folk. How musical that soft brogue of yours, with its unlooked-for stresses and song-like inflections. Your wits, how nimble your discourse. Your hands and features, how lively in narrative. Your feelings, how instantly responsive to the call for laughter or tears – so that life among you is real with the emphasised and heightened reality of a stage play in the hands of skilful actors who never miss their cues or bungle their points. Dear, courteous, hospitable, sensitive folk, if ever I write a word of depreciation – or what you find hardest to pardon, ridicule – of you and your ways, may I never again hear the dulcet voices of Down Along, or taste its ambrosial cream and aromatic saffron buns; or, on its cliffs in March, feast my eyes on the snow and fire of blackthorn and gorse against the deep blue sea and bright blue sky; or in summer breathe the salt-sweet harmony of oar-weed and heather bloom; or feel in autumn the soft prickling caress of Atlantic rains upon my face."

— SIMON PARKER

LINKINHORNE 2002

CHARLES LEE AND THE
NEWLYN SCHOOL

S O MUCH has been written about the Newlyn School
of painters in recent years that it might reasonably be
assumed that little new could be added to the story of
their time in West Cornwall.

It is well documented by Charles Lee himself in the
detailed journals he kept (*The Cornish Journal of Charles
Lee* edited by Ken Phillipps, Tabb House, 1995) that he
was, for some time, part of the Newlyn School fraternity.

Lee lived amongst the likes of Stanhope Forbes, Thomas
Cooper Gotch, Edwin Harris, Henry Rheam, Frank
Bramley, Samuel John Lamorna Birch and Walter Langley.
Yet not one of the many volumes written on the colony and
its members mentions his involvement.

He attended their parties, played piano for their soirées,
and wrote their pantomimes and shows, which were performed at St John's Hall in Penzance. It is tempting even to
wonder whether Lee may have sat for at least one of the
artists, though the probability is that his shyness would
almost certainly have prevented him from doing so. It was
perhaps this same shyness which stopped him being included in any of the group photographs, although in one such
picture there is an unidentified figure with bowler and pipe

standing with Percy Craft, Frank Bodilly, Edwin Harris, Fred Millard, Frank Bramley, Walter Langley, William Fletcher and Albert Chevallier Tayler who is tantalisingly similar to him.

Lee first lodged with Mrs Elizabeth Simons in the end terrace house (now No 86) at the corner of Fore Street, Newlyn in 1891. The occupants of the house, as recorded in the Census of that year, were:

William J Simons, fisherman, 57 years, born Newlyn.

Elizabeth J Simons, wife, 57 years, born Newlyn.

William Simons, son, 23 years, born Newlyn.

Elizabeth T Simons, daughter, 19 years, born Newlyn.

Jane T Badcock, grand-daughter, 6 years, scholar, born Newlyn.

Charles J Lee, boarder, single, aged 21, student in art, born Stockwell, Surrey.

Robert G McKinlay, boarder, single, 19 years, student in art, born Beckinham, Kent.

Lee never credited himself as having a great imagination, and while in one sense this was simple modesty on his part, it is also true that most of his stories, and the characters contained in them, are based on real people and events.

Perhaps it was his kindly nature and ability to integrate without intrusion that led to him being invited to drink with the fishermen at Newlyn hostelries, before strolling across the village to mingle with the fashionable London set, as a guest of Stanhope and Elizabeth Forbes and other members of the Newlyn School. His virtuosity on the piano (he taught the instrument and was later also resident organist at St Mawgan Church) would also have made him a popular guest at such gatherings.

His seldom mentioned novel, *Cynthia In The West*, published in 1900, concerns the lives of a group of famous artists living in a West Cornwall fishing village.

At the beginning of *Cynthia In The West*, the narrator, one Robert Maurice, arrives at a station and is then taken on an hour-long journey by horse and trap to his lodgings in the village. The length of journey and the terrain described along the way has prompted some to conclude that the station could not have been Penzance and the destination was therefore not Newlyn. But that would surely be taking Lee's supposed lack of imagination too far, the described journey being simply a literary device by which to introduce the character of the driver, Sampy, and to allow him to opine on the peculiar ways of artists.

Lee was well acquainted with the members of the group, and while it would be foolish to conclude that *Cynthia In The West's* central character, George Forester, was entirely based on Stanhope Forbes and that Cynthia was his wife Elizabeth, or that Jack Gibbs was perhaps Thomas Cooper Gotch or Otto Trist was Walter Langley, it seems inconceivable that Lee, especially considering his self-professed lack of imagination, would choose to invent an entire colony of famous painters in another port when he had lived among a real colony of eminent artists at Newlyn.

Newlyn, therefore, is Tregurda in this instance and the artists described in *Cynthia In The West* must, in large part, be drawn from the Newlyn School of painters present in the village at that time. Compare, for example, Lee's diary description of Forbes with that of Forester in *Cynthia In The West*.

Lee's journal entry dated 10th December 1892 reads: "Last night at the Gotches again. Met Mr and Mrs Stanhope Forbes. He is littlish, slight and dark, with clear-cut aquiline features, something like Charles Lamb. He gesticulates when talking, and his talk is copious, discursive and a little wearisome. He tells stories with all the excessive detail of a charwoman. Very pleasant though, and so is his wife."

This, in turn, is the fictional Robert Maurice's first impression of Forester: "Maurice's eyes returned to Forester. So that was George Forester. They said the Academy doors were ajar to receive him. They told a story of obscure genius accidentally discovered behind the counter of a provincial shop, led forward by a helping hand, trained a little and praised a great deal, and remaining unspoiled alike by praise and by training. So that was Forester. Not a handsome face, certainly, but attractive by a kind of reserved strength. The eyes did not seem to belong to it; they were the large, brown, liquid eyes of some animal – a tame deer, say. 'He dreams and he acts,' said Maurice to himself. Nothing about him betrayed a humble origin. He wore correct evening dress, and wore it comfortably; he was neither awkward nor self-conscious; yet somehow he seemed out of place where he was."

Later, he writes: "No special memory of the table talk remains with Maurice, except that Mrs Wilmington, for some reason of her own, devoted especial attention to the task of drawing Forester out and keeping him in prominence – not without a certain measure of success. True, she could not lend him eloquence, but it was evident that Forester in a small circle of quiet conversation was not the tongue-tied Forester of the chattering crowd. Appealed to for opinions on this and that, he floundered grievously, but the tale of a fishing adventure was told with positive animation."

Leaving aside the Forbes/Forester theory, it is important to establish whether it is possible that Lee's Tregurda is the artists' Newlyn. And it would appear, at first, that the timescale does not fit the facts.

Lee's notes from 15th September 1898 place him in Portloe, where an extract from his journals includes a section on landing a haul of pilchards. This piece was later "worked up", as Lee would say, for a scene in *Cynthia In The West*. So, if he was still writing *Cynthia In The West* during 1898 (which he clearly was, as shown by the journal extract), the year *Paul Carah Cornishman* was published and a year after *The Widow Woman* first appeared, why does it seem so crude and unpolished compared to the already published works?

The answer probably lies in the unexpected success of *The Widow Woman* and *Paul Carah*, which fuelled such interest in this new voice that his publishers were clamouring for another novel. But without a suitable sequel, Lee may have decided to resurrect a story he had begun when he first arrived in Newlyn, simply adding episodes he had written or gleaned in the intervening years, based on the various Cornish locations he had become acquainted with. *Cynthia In The West* was published in 1900, though in all probability it was written over a period of perhaps eight to ten years.

This is by no means a concrete explanation, but in the absence of any notes from Lee himself, it would appear to be the most likely. It also explains why *Cynthia In The West*, while containing many gems of narrative, lacks the distinctive Lee style of later volumes. And perhaps the most convincing aspect is that the recording of dialect in parts of *Cynthia In The West* is poor, bearing little relation to his other works. Lee's style is uncomfortable, the dialect is patchy and he appears slightly awkward with his craft, even pretentious. The truth is that *Cynthia In The West* was simply the work of a writer who had yet to master his craft and to find his voice.

But find it he did, and it was the voice of the ordinary working people of Cornwall; for while Lee was neither a gentleman or a labouring man, his heart was with the latter. *Cynthia In The West* was the one and only occasion when he set his narrative among the privileged classes – and it ridicules them mercilessly. The only one who escapes is Cynthia, perhaps because Lee was secretly in love with the girl he chose to name after the Greek goddess of the moon, and for whom he provides many romantic lunar references.

One argument put forward against the characters of *Cynthia In The West* being based on the Newlyn School of painters is that the topography of Tregurda does not match that of Newlyn. However, it could, with a little imagination, be Mousehole or, as by the time the book was published in 1900 Lee had stayed in South Cornwall, the physical location might be based on Gorran.

Cynthia In The West, unlike each of his other published works, was never reprinted, and is not even mentioned alongside his other novels in the 1941 collection published by J M Dent. Could it be that Lee himself, ever sensitive to criticism, realised that it did not match up to his other work and chose to consign the story to those precious few first edition copies?

We might never know, but what *Cynthia In The West* does is allow us an insight into the relationships between the people of Newlyn and their artistic visitors. I prefer to believe that George Forester is largely based on Stanhope A Forbes, the leader of the colony. If this is so, it paints a picture of a man who felt deep respect for his Cornish hosts. And it would seem that this sense of respect was mutual, though it did not extend to all of the members of the colony. In this extract, Sampy, the trap driver, gives his view of Forester.

"See that house 'pon the right? That's where Mr Forester live. Now he's deffrant. Maybe you know Mr Forester, young man?"

"I have heard of him," said Maurice. "They think a lot of Mr Forester up in London."

"Do they now? So do we down to Tregurda. A lot we think av'm. He's what we call a gentleman, Mr Forester is. Quiet – none av your slap-the-man-on-the-back, chuck-the-maid-under-the-chin chaps, like Mr Gibbs, but a quiet unashuming young feller, that you feel drawed to, to once. He's a gentleman, and yet he make us feel he's one av us, if you ondershtand. So they think a lot av Mr Forester up to London church town? That's very well."

"Yes," said Maurice. "His pictures, you know–"

Sampy waved his whip.

"Pickshers? 'Tedn' the pickshers; 'tis the man! Don't say much, but lean up agin a boat alongside av 'm for five minutes, and he's your friend. Not a crook in him – straight as a willow, gentle as a maid; don't say much, but say what he mean – that's Mr Forester. He's a man you can be dependent on. Worth the lot av 'em, says Sampy."

This respect, admiration and affection is reciprocated by Forester who, after the snooty Wilmingtons and other members of the colony had mocked the "primitive and uncouth" ways of Tregurda people, speaks out in their defence.

"I think," he said, "I think that you – we – are hardly just to these people. They are good people; they live hard lives. The men take their lives in their hands daily; the women have much to bear. I could tell stories: there is suffering; they are too proud to reveal it. Their ways may seem absurd – I know I am deficient in humour; but I think that, knowing them better, one would cease to laugh at them. I have learned to respect them deeply. They have no time to sit and look at Nature. Their life is one long fight with her. This painting as a life-work – it is playing at living. They live. I am ashamed sometimes. The other day I was starting for a sail with Tom Blamey, and one of the old men said to me, 'All very well for you, Mr Forester, but to my mind, the man who goes to sea for pleasure would go to hell for pastime'."

This extract comes from a chapter entitled *Forester Speaks*, but like so much of Lee's work, what he is actually doing, through the character of Forester, is very clearly nailing his own true colours firmly to the mast and indicating for which camp he feels the greatest allegiance. And he galvanises his position elsewhere, as in this extract, also from *Cynthia In The West*:

"Jack Gibbs' confession of his failure to get on with the villagers was not surprising. To the Cornish fisherman, with his courteous independence and his sensitive pride, an assumption of superiority and a condescension to familiarity are things equally distasteful."

It only seems fair at this point to let Stanhope Forbes, who stands accused of being Lee's model for George Forester, to speak for himself on his relationship with the people of his adopted home in Newlyn. For this we can turn to his illuminating portrait of the life of the port, *A Newlyn Retrospective*, published in Sir Arthur Quiller Couch's *Cornish Magazine* of 1898.

"When one considers the interest aroused by our proceedings, it speaks well for the good nature of the village folk that I can scarcely ever remember asking permission to set up my easel without it being freely accorded. Indeed, it is fortunate for us that the relations of the artists to the villagers have always been so cordial and satisfactory. The people intelligently grasped the idea that there was nothing derogatory to their being painted – indeed, saw and felt the implied compliment. And what better material could artists have wished for? A fine-knit race of men and women, engaged in a healthy and picturesque occupation, and one which by its nature gives the painter his opportunity, when storms and tempests arise, to secure the necessary sittings; swarms of children, many charmingly pretty; no wonder that enough material has been found to keep us engaged these many years. Nothing could exceed the good nature with which the village folk came to regard behaviour which might well have been thought intrusive on the part of any others than the members of our craft."

———⟶•◦•⟵———

On several occasions in the course of his writing Lee pokes fun at the artists' trade, not only in *Cynthia In The West*, but also in *Paul Carah*.

In *Cynthia In The West*, Sampy pulls no punches in his condemnation of these creative visitors.

"Artists! And they call it working! I've seed them at it. One dab, two dabs, jump back a yard, head on showlder and eyes scriffed up. Jump for'ard again, rub out what you've done. Off hat, set down, light your pipe, puff, puff, for ten minutes. Up agin, stick your thumb in the hole av the machine, dab, dab, twiggle, splash. Two minutes, and up you jump once more. How's that? Shake head, and out with your backy-pooch – 'nother spell, b'lieve. 'Work?' says I to one av 'em one day, 'Tell 'ee what 'tis, mister, I'd like to see you paint a house, paint en inside and out – but I shouldn' like to be the man that's waiting to move into that house'.

"That's what I said to'm, and he hadn' a word to say back to Sampy. And when they'm done, these picksher edn' much account, to my mind – not much account, they edn'. I've got a picksher home – grocer sent en last Christmas – owld man setting by the fire smoking, owld woman knitting opposite. Very pretty 'tis – and that smooth and finished off! Many's the time I've counted the stitches on that owld girl's needle. Ess, that picksher'll bear some looking into, b'lieve.

"But these chaps yonder – well, when they say the picksher's done, you must take their word fur'n, and stand two yards off and look at en through the corner av your eye. 'Tedn' so bad then; but come close, and 'tedn' no picksher 'tall – 'tis nothing but a mask av onreasonable paint. And that thick, you want to take a plane and smooth it down.

"And as for finish! Look now. Mr Gibbs, he painted a picksher last year – picksher av a gate 'twas, and a man standing by. Gate was all right – drawed off proper, that gate was – five bars all complete, as pretty a gate as ever I see. But the man! If you'll believe me, that man hadn' got no face – no nose, no mouth, no eyes, no nothing – just a dollop av yaller paint. Now I ask you, young chap, how didn' Mr Gibbs give that poor mortal a face?"

Disclaiming all competence to pronounce on a question of art, Maurice suggested that perhaps Mr Gibbs didn't want to distract the spectator's attention from the gate.

"Dishtruct my attention!" exclaimed Sampy. "That's just what it do! 'Tis clean dishtruction and ruin to my attention, so fur's the gate go. When Sampy see man without a face, Sampy want to know what's up with him. Lev the gate swing or hang, my mind's on the man. I wouldn' have that picksher in my house, not for a thousand pounds. Gashly, I call en."

A similar view is expounded by Jog'fry Jose, when he says to Paul Carah: "Some do come in here, an' say to me, 'Ben, how don't 'ee have stately pictures 'pon your walls, like we, 'stead o' these bistly auld maps?' But what I say is – maps do always tell the truth; there edn' no deception in maps, they're sound doctrine all the while. But pictures – pictures are lyin' trade, an' meant to deceive the eye.

"Take a picture of a place – Porthvean, say – an' look upon 'm. Brave an' pretty, say you, an' wonderful like; might be the auld town itself. But 'a edn' no s'ch thing, I say – edn' but a pretence an' a deception. An' 'a don't tell 'ee nothin' – don't give 'ee no manner of information – don't give 'ee nothin' but just what you can see for yourself. 'Which is Fisherman's Arms and which is Wesley Chapel?' you ask. Picture waan't tell 'ee. What's the use of en, I ask?

"Pictures! I d'knaw all about 'em; I've seed 'em concoctin'. There was a young artis' chap goin' round laast summer with his paintin' tayckle, an' I used to keep an eye 'pon 'm. Well, you wouldn' believe! The scand'lous way that chap 'ud go alterin' an' improvin' the Lord's handi-work, puttin' in a tree here, an' missin' out a stone there, an' manufacturin' sheep an' things out of his own brain! I'd say to him, 'How come you put trees there where there edn' none?' 'That's to improve the composition,' he say. 'Young man,' I says to 'm, 'simmin' to me, drawing lies is 'most as bad as tellin' 'em.'

"That made en laff fit to scat his sides. But I knawed I was right. No lyin' pictures for me. I stick to maps."

An interesting contribution Lee made to the life of the Newlyn colony was in the writing of musical shows, the proceeds from which were donated to the Newlyn Artists Dramatic Society and other charities. Those taking part in the public entertainments included Edwin Harris, Thomas Cooper Gotch, John da Costa, Henry Rheam, John Crooke, Frederick Evans, Percy Craft, Walter Langley, Samuel Green Enderby, WHA Theed, AR Davies, Charles Trevor Garland, Ernest Robert Ireland Blackburne, Lionel Birch and Fred Hall (Could these be the real Jack Cecil Mauleverer Gibbs, Ethel Ralston, Otto Trist, Brent, Cynthia Paget, Harry and Alice Wilmington, Dora Murdoch, George Forester, and Vincent of *Cynthia In The West*?), with Lee credited as musical director and composer.

There is a surviving poster for one of these concerts, which reads: "On no account attend the Dark Seance to be held at St John's Hall, Penzance on March 5th and 6th 1894 at 8pm by that unique little lot of Unartistic Incapable Aboriginal Amateurs known to the police as Lubly Lobengula's Impecunious Impi. Greatest efforts will be made to provide a dull and uninteresting programme. All vocal and instrumental music strictly out of time and tune. Horrible tortures will be inflicted on the audience."

⟶•⟨

So, were the characters in *Cynthia In The West* based on the members of the Newlyn School of painters in the early 1890s? It seems certain, and perhaps in the following line Lee himself intended to give us a fairly strong clue: "That was the way with all my stuff; my powers of invention were practically non-existent."

— SIMON PARKER
LINKINHORNE 2002

CHARLES LEE – A CRITICAL VIEW

WHAT SETS Charles Lee apart from other writers of his time, or subsequently, was his ability to record dialect. And it is perhaps dialect that is at the root of his relative obscurity.

Anne Treneer, author of *Schoolhouse in the Wind* and *Happy Button*, was a master of her dialect; but she, like Lee, still does not enjoy the status of authors writing in the "Queen's English".

There is, perhaps, a reluctance on the part of many readers to engage in the vernacular. But this is a mistake. Lee's style, like Treneer's, is cleverly executed so that it does not exclude readers who possess no knowledge of Cornish dialect.

As the Times Literary Supplement put it: "There is nothing in Lee's dialect to estrange the English reader; the sketches and short stories show the now rare conviction that the way to reveal character is through narrative, not analysis."

A L Rowse agreed, stating: "There is hardly a thing that one would question in his usage of dialect."

And for anyone who has grown up in Cornwall, Lee's characters only serve to heighten that strong sense of identity and distinctiveness which stirs Cornish people's emotions. Ken Phillipps expressed this emotion perfectly in his book, *Catching Cornwall in Flight*, when he wrote: "An entity does not prove to be a Cornish nation if one has to go to Twickenham, or Tottenham, or somewhere else to assert this."

And he added: "Often a word or two of dialect is worth a pound or two of exposition in standard English. And Charles Lee's *The Widow Woman* is no surer documentation for West Cornwall speech."

The point of dialect is to create a true picture. Lee's stories would stand on their own in any language, such is their charm and humour, but that would be to miss the point of Lee's intentions. Without the authentic tongue of the Cornish man, woman and child, they would lose their unique quality.

The Cornish are different. Their language is different and so is their dialect, and some things peculiar to the Cornish psyche – the idiosyncratic humour, the pride, the in-your-face irreverence – simply cannot be expressed in standard English.

This dedication to the diligent and accurate reproduction of dialect is a quality that distinguishes him from other writers of his age and one which should endear him especially to Cornish readers. At a time when Victorian Britain was in the grip of a rigid regime of respectability and conformity, where rural dialects were considered uncultured, Charles Lee was concentrating his thoughts on the outpourings of one Elizabeth Pollard, a bearded fishing boat owner in search of romance, and the central character of his first novel, *The Widow Woman*.

Lee probably observed that with the coming of the railway to the far west, the dialects of Cornwall were already on the wane. And perhaps he was intending, through his novels, not only to be a successful author, but to be remembered as a social documenter. The dialects of Cornwall are far from dead, but their usage has diminished significantly since Lee's time.

As Ken Phillipps so succinctly put it in *Catching Cornwall In Flight*: "Dialect does not die out 'all at once' of course; it is more like the former villages and towns on the East Anglian coast, like Dunwich, for example, that gradually are eroded and disappear into the sea."

<hr>

We know that apart from a few pantomime scores for productions in Letchworth Garden City, Lee's true muse was Cornwall. But while he may not have been sufficiently inspired by his new home in Hertfordshire to pen another novel, that does not explain why he did not continue to draw on his experiences in Cornwall for subject matter.

All of which leaves two important questions unanswered: Why did he stop writing and why is he not remembered? Shy, self-effacing, awkward in company and without an idea of how to promote his own work, Charles Lee was a maverick. But for a short period from the 1890s to the early years of the 20th Century, he was a prolific author. In addition to the five novels – *The Widow Woman, Our Little*

Town, Paul Carah Cornishman, Dorinda's Birthday and *Cynthia In The West* – and a string of short stories and plays, his pantomimes were said to rival Noel Coward for their satirical wit.

He was cheered by the likes of Walter de la Mare, Heath Robinson, Wyndham Lewis and the Newlyn School of painters (see chapter Charles Lee and the Newlyn School), to name but a few, and received glowing reviews in literary magazines and newspapers.

So the puzzling question is why he gave up writing so suddenly and completely to take a job as a proof reader of other, mostly lesser, writers' work at J M Dent.

It is true that his last novel, *Dorinda's Birthday*, was less than well received, though Sir Arthur Quiller Couch later compared it in quality to the greats. In his introduction to the 1941 collection, *Cornish Tales*, Q wrote: "In 1911 Mr Lee produced *Dorinda's Birthday*, the neglect of which little masterpiece reflects discredit alike on the reviewers and the reading public of that day. For a masterpiece it is; a fair rival to Mrs Gaskell's *Cousin Phyllis* and Thomas Hardy's *Under The Greenwood Tree*."

The parallels here with Hardy's decision to abandon novel writing in favour of poetry in the wake of damning reviews of *Jude The Obscure* are marked. And while Lee did not have to endure such savage comments as "depraved" and "drivel" as Hardy did, it seems highly likely the poor reception of *Dorinda's Birthday* had a profound effect on his confidence.

However, in the absence of an explanation from Charles

Lee himself, we must rely on some melancholy remarks he made in a letter to E F Bozman, his employer at J M Dent, and a recent statement from his former housekeeper, Glyn Jones, who told me: "He stopped writing because no one recognised his talents. I think he felt this for the rest of his life."

A combination of mild depression, a lack of self confidence and one adverse review, it seems, deprived the world of forty years of writing talent. Recurring poor health – the reason for his first visits to Cornwall – also seems likely to have been a contributory factor in his decision. His publishers were keen for more, and yet he did not feel confident even to offer them his already completed stories.

These shorter works, contained in this volume, are set in Newlyn, St Mawgan, Coverack and Portloe; they remained unpublished until now, despite their obvious literary merits. Among them are some of Lee's most valuable works, not only for lovers of fine literature and a good yarn, but also for those concerned with Cornish social history of the late Victorian and early Edwardian eras.

The purpose of presenting this collection of "lost" stories is twofold: to provide enjoyment to a new generation of readers who may come to appreciate the great contribution Charles Lee has made to Cornish writing, and secondly to rekindle interest in this forgotten hero of Cornish literature and elevate him to his rightful place among the greats.

Perhaps the most significant piece among this collection is *Mrs Tonkin at Home*. It is a dramatic and characteristically witty description of the house where Lee lodged in

Newlyn and from where he gathered material for his classic *The Widow Woman*. Mrs Tonkin was in fact his landlady, Mrs Elizabeth Simons. In the story, Lee describes the house with its net loft and barking pit, the Simons family, and the comings, goings and "coozings" in Green Street, Newlyn in the 1890s. He writes with sincerity, charm and compassion, painting an accurate portrait of the time.

Mrs Simons would say to visitors: "Don't take no notice of Mr Lee, he's a writer."

And anyone who doubts the link between real people in Cornish communities and Lee's fictional characters need look no further than Mrs Simons herself, who must have provided much of the inspiration for the central character in *The Widow Woman*.

His characterisation was astute and masterly, and while Mrs Simons was not the widow Elizabeth Pollard in real life (this honour goes to Mrs Simons' friend, Mary Pollard, who Lee described in his journal of 19th December 1892 as being "built on the grand scale"), it is fair to say that she provided the framework for her character and that of a number of Lee's other female characters. It might even be argued that had Lee lodged in a less entertaining household than that of Elizabeth Simons he may not even have embarked on creating his Cornish tales. One can imagine if Lee was ever at a loss as to how to structure a piece of dialogue for a character, he would need only to imagine how Mrs Simons might express herself in such a situation.

Elizabeth Simons and her husband William (who is recorded by Lee in his journal as saying: "I've lived on the say and by the say all my life, but I hate the sight of 't and I hate the sound of 't. Inland's where I'd like to live, Muster Lee, 'mong the trees, where nawthen 'ud meet my sight but trees and green herbs. Out o' sight and hearing o' the say for ever and ever – that's where I'd like to be') were the great grandparents of Newlyn writer, journalist, singer and Bard of the Gorsedd, Douglas Williams. Douglas takes up the story: "My mother, Hannah Williams, was born in 1898, five years after Charles Lee left, but she told me that her family would often tell her and others of the time Lee spent with them and how he would spend hours sitting quietly in the corner by the window. What he was doing was carefully writing down the conversations, with accents and dialects, as the neighbours popped in for a chat with the Simons family. And so, instead of writing whatever they imagined, he would be getting a perfect picture of everything going on. I have always thought, and still do, that the language in *The Widow Woman* is the nearest a writer has got to capturing the Newlyn 'chat'."

Lee would sit silently unnoticed for hours, jotting down the way the local people thought and spoke. *The Widow Woman* came out of this study, as did *Mrs Tonkin at Home*, and it is likely some of the characters and situations in *Paul Carah*, though set in Coverack, may also have been inspired by Newlyn people.

Coming from a cultured, though not wealthy background he was able to take people into his confidence. This ability to mingle comfortably and gain the friendship of those from every strata of what was then a class-ridden society was one of his great strengths. It is significant that whereas many another writer of the time arrogantly bathed in their own perceived superiority over the ordinary, working people of Cornwall, Lee was the innocent, in awe and envy of their seemingly uncluttered lives and closeness to nature and the elements. This is illustrated in this passage from *Penhaligon and Galatea* in which the narrator is desperate to escape the talk of the artists.

"The place suited me exactly. Engaging a woman to come up daily and see to the cooking and tidying, I settled steadily to work, undisturbed by art-chatter and musical evenings and the rest of the nonsense. Of course I couldn't do without society altogether, but if the stranger knows how to conduct himself with decency and respect he will never lack entertaining company in the Duchy. 'Bumpkin' is the last word to apply to the Cornish rustic, with his courteous manners, his alert Celtic wit, and his shrewdly humourous outlook on life."

This natural skill enabled him accurately and sensitively to record the mannerisms and speech of Cornish working people like no other. There is a popular tale that when *The Widow Woman* was first published the characters were so easily identifiable as to cause offence, and that Lee was made to feel unwelcome in the port. But there is no real evidence for this, apart from a comment attributed to Lee in which he is supposed to have told the painter Thomas Cooper Gotch he feared he may have upset some people. The general view, however, is that he was held in great esteem by most local people.

Incidentally, the reason for his choice of the name Elizabeth Pollard as the central character in *The Widow Woman* can be found in *The Vale of Lanherne*; it is typical of Lee's humanity and was his way of immortalising the name of a person who had lived such a poor and hard life. The real Elizabeth Pollard died in St Mawgan in 1711 after many years of receiving relief from the parish. Her burial expenses came to £1 2s 6d, and to defray these the overseers had her goods sold. There is a memorandum of the old lady's possessions in the parish accounts, which reads: "One bed furnished, three bras (sic) pans, two pewter dishes, one cage, one curne (a hand mill for grinding corn), one pare (sic) of wool cards." Lee found this tale immensely moving, lamenting the fact that the woman did not even possess a chair, and that her entire estate was sold for just £1 10s.

Lee was again fishing for true Cornish voices during his stay at Portloe, the setting for his masterpiece, *Our Little Town*, a series of wickedly funny and accurately observed vignettes of local life. His characters are so believable that it seems certain they were all based on real inhabitants of the fishing port, or at least transported from other villages in Cornwall. *Our Little Town* seems to particularly explain why Lee should over-modestly assert that his powers of invention were "practically non-existent".

One of the chief characters in the book is Penticost, a curmudgeonly soul who runs the cobbler's shop – the chief meeting place of the male population – in the village of Porthjulyan (Portloe). A Portloe man, Fred Johns, who was born in 1898, the year Charles Lee stayed in the village, told me some years ago that when he was a boy there was a well-known one-legged shoemaker called William Rundle, whose shop was a gathering place for men to talk, relax, smoke and discuss the affairs of the day. The position and description of Mr Rundle's shop fits that of Lee's Penticost's. And the similarities do not end there.

Both William Rundle and Penticost are staunch Wesleyans, taken to quoting religious tracts at will. A sign hangs in Penticost's shop, which reads: "No swearing. No damning. No religion except for Penticost – he can't help it. No wimin alowd. No more than five to smoke to once. No taking wax-ends without permission." It would seem probable that this sign, or one much like it, really hung in Rundle's shop.

Lee changed the names of his characters for obvious reasons, but it is less clear why he chose to invent the names of the locations. It has not been possible to identify every town and village featured in his stories, but here are a few:

The Widow Woman – Pendennack – Newlyn
Paul Carah, Cornishman – Porthvean – Coverack
Cynthia In The West – Tregurda – Newlyn/Mousehole, though the physical setting seems closer to Gorran, of which Lee was well acquainted
Our Little Town – Porthjulyan – Portloe
A Strong Man – Portrewan – Cadgwith
The White Bonnet – St Mawgan in Pydar
The Lucubrations of Thyrza Theophila – St Kenna – Truro
Langarrock Great Tree – Langarrock – St Mawgan in Pydar
Wisht Wood – possibly The Dizzard

Dorinda's Birthday – Sunny Corner, between Porthmellan and St Hender Churchtown in the Nanheviock Valley – a charmed and perhaps invented location between Mawgan Porth and St Mawgan in Pydar

<hr />

Why *Chasing Tales*? Those expecting cynical analysis may have been disappointed by this trio of biographical introductions – but this study was born of admiration and love; it is, essentially, a celebration of Charles Lee's life and work.

The title, *Chasing Tales*, was chosen for two reasons. Firstly, Lee was himself a collector of stories, characters, incidents, anecdotes, situations, locations, and in fact anything he thought he could later "work up", as he put it in his journals, into the basis of a narrative. In the pursuit of a plot or personality he would patiently wait, observe and record.

Secondly, as any biographer knows, to do their subject justice it is necessary to look beyond the bare facts, the clues deliberately left behind in letters and other correspondence, and to attempt to think like the subject himself, to try and get inside his mind.

In Lee's case this was not difficult, and the single most decisive factor which led to what some might consider a somewhat "anorak-like" quest on my part was that from the moment I picked up *The Widow Woman* I felt a deep affinity with Lee, his style of writing, his outlook, his loves, his opinions, his contempt for authority. It is something I have not experienced as strongly with any other writer before or since.

It was back in the 1980s, while researching the story of the Newlyn fishing riots of 1896, that I first encountered the world of Charles Lee. And I am indebted to Jan Ruhrmund, who was then working in a Penzance rare book shop, for suggesting I read *The Widow Woman*, as it is set in Newlyn at about the same time as the riots. She said she would look out for a copy and, by chance, that same day one was offered to her.

And so began the long quest..... chasing tales.

—————➤◆◄—————

Glyn and Dorothy Jones of Letchworth Garden City came to inherit the Lees' entire house and contents. The couple lived in Charles' house, Lanvean, for many years after Olive's death. Glyn has now agreed to give what remains of Lee's papers to the Royal Cornwall Museum in Truro.

— SIMON PARKER
LINKINHORNE 2002

THE PIGS OF ST KERVAN

S T KERVAN Churchtown always was a terrible place for pigs. Everybody kept them, and everybody was downright mazed about them – couldn' talk o' nothing else, hardly. Didn' matter what subject you pitched with a St Kervan man – politics, crops, state of your health, religion – whatever 'a was, he'd begin working the discourse round, till in two minutes you'd be hearing all about the old sow and her last litter, or how much the fat hog weighed when 'a was cut up.

And the way they'd talk, you wouldn' believe. I mind meeting Susan Jolly one day, and she was looking some bad, sure enough.

"You'm looking poorish, Susan," I said.

"Ess, well," says she, "I an't feeling very well, that's true, nor Jim, my 'usband, he an't feeling very well, nor none of the fam'ly haven' been feeling very well just lately, not since the pig was killed. We was terrible attached to the pig, Mr Hoskyn."

Well, about five years ago, St Kervan men started a club for insuring their pigs agin fever and sickness. Everything in proper form – Parson Kessel for chairman, Jenkin, the schoolmaster, for vice, somebody told off to keep accounts, somebody else for hon'rary medical adviser, and a general meeting once a quarter in the schoolroom. Every pig in the place entered his name 'pon the books and paid his sub-scription like a man, and being a healthy time with pigs just then, 'twasn' long before they'd got a tidy thirty pound to their credit up to the bank, and all the world heard tell of that tidy thirty pound till all the world was sick of it, you may be sure.

Now we've a considerable few down here to Port Oliver that keep pigs too. We an't passionate about 'em, but still, in a moderate way, and no sentiment, Port Oliver's as pig-gish a locality as you'll find anywhere. Well, one day a St Kervan man was down here peacocking away about his pigs, and all of their pigs, and the grand surplus up to the bank, and the wonderful things they were going to do with it, and the rest of the yarn that we knowed without book. So when he'd gone, one of our chaps up and said: "I'm about sick of this. 'Tis time Churchtown pigs was stopped from crowing over their betters. I move we start a club of our own down here."

"Wait a bit," said I. "You don't sink a well when you've got a river flowing by your door. Here's a old-established and prosperous institution up to Churchtown. Let's behave neighbourly, and patronise the same."

So after talking of it over, we agreed to send up a depy-tation next week, when the pig club's committee meeting was due. So we made up our depytation – me at the head, and two stout wrestling chaps to back me up in case of argyment – and when the night come, off we go and meet the delegates of the Churchtown pigs in the schoolroom. Presently the chairman calls upon Mister Jacob Hoskyn, and up I get and state the case for our poor unprovided pigs – put it plain and straight. Any objections? Seemingly no.

"Very well," said I. "That's our case. Put it to the vote, Mr Chairman, and leave us go home-along to supper."

"Hold on a bit!" says a holler voice, and up jump old Josiah Rickard. Never was such a chap as 'Siah for smelling out a roguery where nobody else could.

"Beware!" says he. "Be on your guard, Churchtown men! Our pigs is well-behaved pigs. They keep to their com-for'ble little homes all the while. But these Port Oliver pigs, they'm vaggybonds – low vaggybonds and fly-by-nights, prowling around all the time, and nobody looking after them. And what's the result?" hollers 'Siah, hammering 'pon the table.

"Where's Archie Dunstone's sow and her tender young fam'ly? Food for fishes, every one! Over cliff they went to their doom one stormy night, as you all do know. What's come to Ben Truscott's fat hog, that was going to get the prize over our heads next cattle show? What's come to him, I say? Bacon, be-george! Bacon he've come to before his time, with his neck broke by a cart-wheel, along of his lying across the road after dark, and couldn' get up in time, and his fat betrayed him.

"Men of St Kervan," says Josiah, "this here club of ourn, 'tis a sick-club – 'tisn' no accident insurance company. This here proposal an't nothing but a low scheme to put our pigs' hard-earned thirty pound into the rascally pockets of these Port Oliver swine. So, Mr Chairman," says he, "I move to reject the supplication, without Port Oliver do agree to put padlocks on every sty door, and no pigs allowed out after dark 'pon no consideration."

"Never!" said I. "This here's a free country, and Cornish pigs ben't to be treated like they was heathen slaves."

"Very well then," says Josiah agin. "Pay tribble rates, and we'll vote your pigs illegible 'pon the books. But not else, be-george." And down he sit.

Well, I looked round 'pon the rest, and I could see by their faces there wasn' no hope for our pigs after what Josiah had said. But I wasn' going off without a quip, you may be sure.

So I said: "Very well. You say our pigs are a flighty lot, and I'm grieved to allow you'm right. Their moral edication have been neglected something terrible, but we'm going to put that square, and then there won't be no more objections, I trust. Mr Jenkin," I said to schoolmaster, "would 'e mind lending us your pig to take home for a few days?"

"Lend 'e my pig" says Jenkin. "How?" says he.

"Why," I said, "to larn our pigs how to behave. Chuckfull of maxims and careful doctrine that pig of yourn should be, feeding of him like you do 'pon old copy books."

And then I put up my hand to our chaps and out we march.

But there an't no pig club up to St Kervan nowadays. You've heard tell of the great storm and flood last Christmas twelvemonth? We had en pretty and bad down here, but nothing to what 'a was up Churchtown way – slates flying, chimney pots falling, and the river gone

50

mazed and dancing a courant down the street. Presently the word came that Jacka's Meadow was flooded – Pigs Corner they mostly called en, because they that hadn' got no gardens used to keep their pigs there. There was a reg'lar terrace of pigsties down by the river in that meadow, and one of 'em belonged to Henrietta Tidy, widow of Phil Tidy, that used to fish down here.

When Henrietta got the news that Pigs Corner was in danger, up she jump, and begin holl'ing: "Aw, my poor Philip!" – Philip being the pig that she'd named for her dead husband because he'd got a look in his eyes that minded her of the poor beauty, so she said. "Aw, my poor Philip! He'll be drownded! Drownded in his bed! I must save en!" – and down she snatch her bonnet from the door.

"Mother"! Says her daughter Annie. "The river's up waist-high! You'll be drownded yourself if you do go!"

"I must save en!" says Henrietta, and out with her dead man's sea-boots, on with 'em, gown tucked up, and off to the door.

"Mother!" cries Annie. "The slates are flying like hail! If one should hit 'e, twill scat your brain abroad!"

"Save en I must!" says Henrietta. Off go her bonnet, on go the copper saucepan instead, like one of these old antikities they used to fight in, and out she go, a strange figure sure enough. Down street she go and into the meadow, splash, splash, and presently she could hear the poor pigs a-screeching.

"I'm a-coming, Philip!" she hollers. "Mother's a-coming, my worm!"

When she got down to the place, there's Philip standing on his hind legs up agin sty door, with the water up to his neck.

"Week!" says he.

"Mother's here, my angel," says she, and she hitched en up somehow 'pon the roof. And then she stayed by en half the night, talking soft to en, so's to keep his heart up, till the water begun to go down. And then home-along she go in her sea boots and saucepan, singing like a lark, so they tell me.

Next day there's grave news going round about the pig that lived next door to Philip. Whether 'twas the fright, or whether 'twas inflammation catched by standing in water up to his nose-ring half the night, that pig was doomed. And whose pig should 'a be but Josiah Rickard's, no less? – and 'Siah in a dreadful way, as you may well suppose. But 'twasn' no use grieving. Everybody said the same thing: that pig must be killed 'pon the spot, for fear 'a should die a nat'ral death. So 'Siah went off to sarch for Barker Boase, the pig-killer, and found en up to the inn, drinking rum hot, same as 'a gen'rally was.

"Barker Boase," says Josiah, "rise up from thy liquor, take thy knife and killing-stool, and go put an end to the pains of my poor suffering pig."

So Barker got up and went off to let Josiah's pig into the Great Secret. 'Siah hadn' the heart to go with him, so he stayed behind and drowned his grief in a noggin. That's where he made a mistake. Barker's legs were stiddy enough, and his hand was stiddy enough, but his brain was a bit woolly, like, and what with the two sties being next door to each other – a pair of semi-detached sties they were – and what with 'Siah's pig and Henrietta's Philip being brothers at birth and the very dapse of each other, Barker got mixed up between 'em, and what should 'a do but cut poor Philip's throat, that Henrietta'd just saved at the risk of her life!

Soon as Barker found out what he'd done, which wasn' till Philip was scalded and scraped, he went off home-along, bolted the door, and went to bed, being the only place that was moderately safe agin a roving widow-woman.

Presently Henrietta came along and hammered 'pon the door and said a few choice words, like, and then she went off and borrowed a boy and a wheelbarrow for to fetch Philip home. A reg'lar procession up the street, so they tell me – first the boy wheeling Philip, stretched out on the barrow all gashly white with a cloth over him, then Henrietta tottering along with her hankercher over her eyes, and Annie walking beside her and putting in a word of comfort now and again. Somebody said Henrietta was wearing her funeral bonnet, but I never did quite believe that.

Next thing that happened was 'Siah going up to Barker's and trying to coax him to go down and kill the right pig. But Barker put his head out window and said he wouldn' stir for nobody's pig, not till Henrietta'd had time to cool down a bit. And no more a' didn' – stopped in bed all day, Barker did, and by next morning Josiah's pig had passed away.

Well, when the next club meeting come on, Henrietta put in a claim for Philip – leastways, not zackly for Philip himself, because she'd got her value out of him in pork already, and he cut up very well, Philip did, but then he wasn' but half grown, and she allowed she'd a right to the other half that would ha' been Philip if he'd lived to be reared.

Some of 'em agreed to that, but others agin said no. The club being a sick club, 'twouldn' do, they said, to go paying out compensation for murder cases. Then Josiah up and put in a claim for his pig. Sick case, sure enough, you'd think, whether you put it down to inflammation or nervous prostration. But some of 'em wanted to argue that 'Siah, having given orders for the pig to be killed, put himself out of court, like, because 'twas his duty then to see the pig was killed without unreasonable delay. Pretty and weak, you'll allow, but some people'll argue 'most anything when their pockets are consarned. There'd been a good deal of swine fever about, you see, and we hadn' heard tell of that grand surplus so much lately.

Anyhow, there they were, disputing away, till at last, when the chairman had used up all his voice-lozenges, he managed to put it to the vote and the majority was for sticking to the cash. So Josiah and Henrietta resigned, and brought an action agin the club. A joint action, 'twas, for being widow-man and widow-woman, and drawed together by their losses and grievances, they'd agreed to make a match of it, set up house together, and knock down the partition between their pigsties.

Well, the action came on, and such a mixed-up old yarn you never heard. Nobody couldn' make nothing of it, not even the lawyers themselves.

So at last the judge up and say: "This beats me. 'Tis my opinion, these two dead pigs are more than the British Constitution can swaller without choking of itself. And so's there shan't be no risk to the nation, I'm going to dismiss the case, and each party to pay his own costs."

Well, that didn' satisfy nobody, as you may suppose. Josiah went about swearing his be-georges that he was going to move for a new trial because he'd found out that the judge was a Jew by the female side, and so couldn' be expected to see fair where pork was consarned. Then his lawyer's bill come in, and 'Siah didn' say no more. Then the club got their bill. Another meeting to discuss the situation. What's the situation? Just enough in the bank to pay the lawyer, five pigs on the sick list, and three of 'em in a bad way. If those pigs should die, what then?

"Then," says chairman, "I'm afraid there'll be nothing for it but a call on the members."

Two minutes after that, there wasn' but only two members left – chairman and vice. All the rest had put in their resignations and walked out. So parson and schoolmaster had a special meeting all to theirselves.

Parson called on schoolmaster to move a resolution dissolving the club. Schoolmaster up and moved it, seconded from the chair. Parson put it to the vote, carried by schoolmaster, and that was the end of the St Kervan Pig Club.

But if you want to make yourself agreeable to a St Kervan man don't so much as mention pork. He's waiting for the word to knock 'e down.

— As told by Jacob Hoskyn of Port Oliver

ANTONY'S QUEST

A NTONY Parkyn was in a prosperous way of business, as carpenter, wheelwright and boat-builder, with a shop and yard down beach and a most comfortable little house in the most select quarter of Porthjulyan.

Well-to-do, good-looking and (at the time of which I write) some way advanced in the thirties, he had yet escaped the fetters of matrimony, to say nothing of the lighter chains that adorn rather than encumber the engaged man; and this is not out of shyness, indifference, or aversion, but from a fastidiousness that can only be described as morbid.

On first emerging into manhood he gave the sex an extended trial, bestowing diligent attention on some half-dozen maids of all shapes and sizes in succession. But he got no profit or entertainment out of any of them.

It may have been sheer ill-luck, but the fact remained that every one of those maidens suffered in her feet with corns, bunions, or the like, which utterly spoiled their action. Antony wouldn't go so far as to say they were foundered altogether, but 'twas a case of cracked heels with them, and no mistake.

Also their conversation was trivial and their demeanour frivolous in the extreme. So he soon abandoned the experiment, and eschewed all thoughts of matrimony for the time.

It was not until the period of my story that he began to consider the matter seriously again. Perhaps he would not have done so even then, but for the death of his widowed mother, an event that left him with a house on his hands and no sister or other female relative available to look after it for him.

The notion of a paid housekeeper did not commend itself to him, and he was reluctantly forced to the conclusion that matrimony was the only alternative. So he set about hunting for a wife, and never since the first institution of wedlock was the search conducted on such thoroughgoing lines. Nothing but the pick of the market would do for him, and it is no exaggeration to say that he ransacked the countryside in pursuit of the eligible article; for a long time with very indifferent success.

At the beginning he threw away an excellent chance or two; for he had never been able to forget his youthful experiences, and on one point he was determined to be satisfied before proceeding any farther. Now a maiden may be ready enough to meet the attentions of a suitor half-way, but the question of corns is much too delicate to introduce into the preliminary stages of the business.

Antony suffered more than one point-blank rebuff before he learned caution in this respect. And in other ways he continued to be hampered by the high standard of perfection he had set up. Take, for example, the episode of Augusta Niles, which I may give in his own words, as he related it an hour afterwards to a large audience down beach. His was an expansive nature; in all his amorous adventures he took the whole town into his confidence, and insisted on our enjoying at second hand the ardours of the chase.

"I see her coming out of chapel," he said, "and somebody said something that made her laugh. 'Well,' said I to myself, 'you ben't much to look at, nor you ben't so young as you was ten year ago, but a prettier cage of teeth I never set eyes on in maid or mare. Them's the teeth for my money,' said I. 'I'd back teeth like those to chaw shoe-leather.'

"So I strolled along after her, keeping my eye 'pon her action, and that seemed all right – stepped out pretty and lively, 'a did. So presen'ly, I catched her up and asked to put her home, and she s'posed I could if I'd a mind to. Well, we talked a bit of this and that, till by-and-by I couldn' think of nothing else to say, though her teeth were chumping away in my brain, like, all the while.

"So I didn' say nothing, nor she nuther, not for a long time, till I happed to glimp' round my nose at her, and just that minute she happed to be glimping round her nose at me, and we turned it off with a laugh, and there was her teeth a-flashing in the sun before my eyes – two rows of reg'lar beauties. So I said – couldn' help myself – 'What handsome teeth you have got, Augusta!' And she said – now what do 'e think she said? – 'So they ought to be,' she said, 'considering father paid six pound for 'em.' My dear life! I went cold all down my back!"

"But where's the harm?" asked an interested auditor. "A valyable young woman, I should say, to carr' six pounds' worth of ivory about with her. Worth more than most of 'em, I reckon."

Antony shook his head. "The maid I marry," he said, impressively, "have got to be a complete Christian, and none of your natural history patchwork. Why, I'd be thinking 'pon the poor dead elephant every time I kissed her!"

Another adventure ended still more disastrously. It may have been humourous, but it certainly was cruel of Sam Jago (our chief of wits) to send Antony tramping five miles up-country on the strength of a glowing description of a maiden whom he (Sam) had seen on his travels, and who, he averred, was the very maid for Antony, from the bucket to the piano.

After a tiresome search, the maiden took final shape as an aged crone, smoking a short clay pipe over a turf fire in a tumble-down hovel. Never dreaming that he had reached his goal, the unsuspecting suitor engaged the lady in conversation; and after some talk at cross purposes it was she who first grasped the situation, and with it the poker, and dashed Antony's hopes in a manner more forcible than polite.

Such setbacks as these might well have deterred another man; but Antony persevered doggedly in his quest of the not impossible she. Systematic in everything, he drew up a list of all the eligible maidens in the district, and pinned it on the wall of his workshop, so that the state of the marriage market was ever before his eyes. From time to time a name would be crossed out, and a note appended, giving briefly the reason for the erasure, thus: Emily Tregilgas (light behaviour in chapel); Susan Beckerleg (courting elsewhere); Mary Drew (three new hats in a fortnit); Annie Pearse (no conversation); Leah Lean (too much to do).

At last, by this careful process of elimination, Antony narrowed down the field of his final choice to two – the sisters Rosie and Emma Hawke. Both were young and comely, sound in wind and limb, and hitherto unappropriated. Each was a touch above the common workaday maiden; Emma had all the artistic dressmaking of the neighbourhood in her hands, and Rosie was mistress of the infant school.

Antony was positive that either the one or the other was the very maid for him; but to decide between them was another matter. After a long and anxious search after one's ideal, to find it in duplicate is surely Fortune's masterpiece in the way of cunning irony. The two dovetailed, so to speak, and together made up Antony's notion of the Perfect Woman.

What was he to do in such a case, for which Christendom provides no adequate solution?

He relished a bit of literature as we say, of an evening. Who could provide it better than Rosie, who, though she habitually conversed in the vernacular when business hours were over, could always turn on her book-English at will, and, moreover, had at her command an inexhaustible stock of fascinating recreative problems, about snails, climbing walls, the price of herrings, wonderful walking and ploughing matches between A and B, and the like – fit for the parlours of the nobility?

Emma pretended to no accomplishments of this dazzling nature; her talents were all of a solid kind. As Antony feelingly observed, a man could be sure his buttons were safe with Emma, and her skill in patching and turning was unrivalled. We have a saying at Porthjulyan to the effect that while any woman can make a new petticoat out of an old skirt, it takes a clever one indeed to fashion a new skirt out of an old petticoat; and even that miracle of sartorial genius, as Antony judged, was not beyond Emma's power.

Such, then, in outline, was the problem Antony set himself to solve. It was further complicated by his original method of courtship, if courtship it could be called. The ordinary procedure of the vacillating suitor would be to walk the maidens out, turn by turn, on alternate Sundays, until such time as blind chance should settle the business with a pregnant glance from a blue eye or a brown, or a distracting glimpse of an ankle at a stile, or a tender, foolish word inadvertently let slip, or some such trivial toy.

But Antony's aims and intentions were all too serious to admit of such haphazard courses. He watched his quarry from afar, and so carefully neglected his opportunities of coming to closer quarters that, if it had not been for his reiterated assurances to third parties, both maidens might well have remained in complete ignorance of his passion.

In order to assist himself in his deliberations, he carried about with him a couple of articles that symbolised, as it were, the attraction and counter-attraction that held him suspended. You would come upon him sitting on the edge of a boat, or pacing up and down a retired corner of the beach, with a pair of scissors in one hand and a pen in the other, absorbed in contemplation of these silent tokens. And as sure as he broached the topic to a confidant, out would come the emblematic tools, to be flourished alternately as he chanted the alternate praises of Emma and Rosie. First, perhaps, he would produce the pen from his breast pocket, gaze at it affectionately, and begin to discourse.

"I see her this afternoon," he might say. "I was passing over by schoolhouse, and I geeked into the window, and there she was, smacking the cheldern's heads. Smacked them all round 'a did, and never missed one out o' the twenty. And that quick and smart! 'Twas like a mason laying on the mortar – flip flap! My life! thinks I. What a mother of a fam'ly that maid would make!"

With a fond sigh he would return Rosie to his pocket, take out Emma, and begin to try her mettle on his fingernails.

"But she's a good one too," he would continue. "'Twas only yes'day I found her young brother poddling about in my shop, where he hadn' no business and been warned off scores of times. So I catched en by the scruff and turned en over 'pon my knee. 'I'll tell my sisters for 'e,' says he. 'Tell away, old cap'n,' says I, and I was just bringing my hand home when I behold a patch let into his li'll burches. Such a patch you never set eyes on; if he hadn' been upsy-down, I'd never ha' knowed 'twas there. And the pretty shape to it,

63

and the way 'twas finished off round the edge – why, 'twas a' ornment, that patch was, a reg'lar ornment! So I said 'James Ernest,' I said, 'tell me true who 'twas put that patch in your li'll burches, and I'll leave 'e go.' So he said 'Antony, hope I may die, 'twas sister Emma put that patch in my li'll burches.' And there's a maid to have in the house!"

And so things went on. One day he would discover some new perfection in Rosie, and the balance would incline in her favour, only to be righted next morning, when some surpassing merit of Emma's was sure to come to light. So far as could be seen, there wasn't a nib or a scissor-blade to choose between the two.

His difficulties might have been lightened had either maid shown a spark of preference for him – he would at least have had a basis of personal discrimination to work from. But sadly, they gave him no cause to hope. It cannot be said that they actually repelled Antony's advances; his Fabian methods did not give them the opportunity.

But in public, at any rate, they were at one in professing the utmost scorn for his pretensions, and the most decided aversion for his person.

Needless to say, Antony was not in the least disconcerted by this. He was not the man to be turned from a set purpose by mere maidenly coyness, whatever exaggerated form it might take. He had sufficient confidence in his own solid merits and in the good sense of his chosen ones to take such feminine flourishes at their proper valuation. Still, there was no denying that the situation was an obscure and complicated one.

What the upshot would have been if he had been left to himself, or whether the scissors or the pen would have carried the day at last, I cannot pretend to guess; for now another hand is laid on the reins of Antony's destiny, and skilfully guides it to an unlooked-for issue.

<hr />

One evening, as Antony on his way home from work was passing, with carefully averted eyes as usual, the abode of his loved ones, he heard a honeyed voice pronounce his name. Looking up, he saw the comely and buxom Widow Hawke standing in the doorway.

"If you don't mind stepping inside for a minute, Antony," said she, "I'd like to have a bit of a chat with 'e."

Antony hesitated, fearing a trap of some sort. For all he knew, Rosie or Emma might be hiding behind the door, ready to fling herself on his neck, and so solve the problem in an altogether arbitrary and irrational fashion.

"The maidens are both out," said Mrs Hawke, almost as if she had guessed the reason of his hesitation.

Thereupon Antony hesitated no longer, but meekly followed her indoors. They sat down. There was nothing formidable in Mrs Hawke's appearance; indeed, she was surprisingly young and good-looking to be the mother of two grown-up daughters. But for all that, Antony felt a slight nervousness, such as any man, even the bravest, might well experience on the occasion of a first formal interview with a potential mother-in-law. But his qualms vanished when Mrs Hawke, with a waggish smile on her face, stooped forward, tapped his knee and said: "Ah Antony, you'm a sad rogue, I fear."

Antony felt flattered, as who would not?

"Don't know how you should think that, Mrs Hawke," he said, modestly.

"Reason why," she replied, "with these two poor maids of mine wearing out their hearts for 'e."

"Aw, come now!" quoth Antony, endeavouring to tuck in the corners of a smile of gratification. "Tidn' so bad as that, I reckon."

"Ay, but 'tis!" insisted Mrs Hawke. "I don't know what to do by them, they're that mopish and vexable. And jalous, too. Won't hardly speak to each other, and when they do, 'tis snap, snap all the while, like congers on a hook. And who's to blame them poor things? Not I, for one."

The gentlest of sighs, the most fleeting of glances, pointed her words. Here was a sensible woman, thought Antony, and straightaway began to unbosom himself. Forth from their sanctuary next his heart came the symbolic pen and scissors, to be laid on the table and toyed with in turn as he elaborately expounded his doubts and difficulties.

"And there 'tis," he concluded. "Capital maids, both of 'em; and here I be between 'em, setting down to a standstill, as you may say."

"Seeming to me, 'tis a case for advice," hinted Mrs Hawke.

"If only you'd help me!" cried Antony eagerly.

"Tis hard for me to do that," sighed she. "They'm capital maids, both, as you do say, and dear loving maids beside, and I'm terrible onwilling to part with ayther one, even to you, Antony, though I couldn' hope for a better son-in-law, not if I had the pick of the land."

"I've just been thinking myself what a fine mother-in-law you'd make," confessed Antony.

"How you do talk!" simpered Mrs Hawke. "Don't know as I ought to listen to 'e when you do talk like that. Seem 'me, you'm a dangerous fellow, Antony."

She paused, and fetched another little sigh. Antony stroked his moustache. Certainly he was a devil of a fellow, and she was a most agreeable woman.

"Some do think Rosie's the prettier-looking one of the two," she resumed, "though I don't see it myself."

"Nor I nuther," agreed Antony. "Edn a pin to choose between them so fur's looks do go. A handsomer pair I never did see."

"Tis a puzzle to me where they get their good looks from," mused Mrs Hawke. "Their father, poor dear beauty, hadn' no more features to him than a dumpy-ball."

Antony reflectively scanned his interlocutor's face. "Must have been from their ma, I reckon," he said at last with sober conviction.

Mrs Hawke tittered, and made as if to throw her apron over her face.

"What a chap you are, with your compliments and nonsense!" she exclaimed. "No wonder the maidens are all mazed after 'e. You get round us women like a hoop round a treacle-cask. But 'tis cur'ous, I allow, the way cheldern do turn arter their parents. Now, there's Emma." She took up the scissors as she spoke, and began skilfully snipping imaginary threads in mid-air. "A smart one with her niddle, as you do know. Well, she get that gift, such as 'tis, from me."

"Sure 'nough!" ejaculated Antony, immensely interested.

"Ess. Never was nobody like me for niddle and thimble when I was a maid. And 'twas niddle and thimble in those days, I can tell 'e; none o' these sewing machines then, to do all the work and leave 'e take all the credit. And when I wadn' stitching and snipping, then I'll be bound you'd find me reading and ciphering; and that's where Rosie do get her love of figures and book-larning from, s'pose."

"That so?" said the dazzled Antony. "I never knowed you was gifted that way, Mrs Hawke."

"I never was one to boast or show off," said Mrs Hawke modestly, as she took up the pen and elegantly flourished invisible signatures over the table-cloth. "And a mother of a family have got other things beside lettratur to see for, what with the meals to get – the maidens never did take to cookery – and the dusting and sweeping to tend to, 'tis a job they hate.

"Though I do make shift now and agin to cut out a pattern for Emma – sewing machine won't help 'e there, Antony – or to put Rosie to rights with a hard sum or the maning of a word she can't make out in her books."

"Tell 'e what 'tis," said Antony in a glow of admiration. "'Tis a pity you didn' have but one daughter and pass it all on to she. Then 'twould be all plain sailing for me. 'Tis my opinion, Mrs Hawke, that your husband that's gone was an oncommon lucky man."

"There you go agin!" cried the lady. "Tis a good job the maidens an't here. Don't know what they'd think to hear e' say such things. Aw well, poor James. Good luck or bad – and 'tid'n for me to say which – he's dead and gone, and I'll never say a word agin him. We've all got our faults, b'lieve, and there's worse faults than temper. That's what I always say when Emma and Rosie get in the tantrums. 'Poor dears' I say, 'who's to blame 'em for what's bred in the bone, like?'"

Antony sat up.

"T-tantrums!" he stammered. "Did-did I onderstand 'e to say tantrums, Mrs Hawke?"

"Law me!" cried Mrs Hawke, with every symptom of horror at her indiscretion. "It slipped out onawares. To think I should say such a thing of my own daughters, and to you of all people! Well, p'raps they may be a bit hot and sharp, but 'tis soon over, I assure 'e. They'll give and take a slap or two, or smash a saucer, or tear up a hank'cher, or some little thing like that, and 'tis all worked off in a minute, and like lambs the rest o' the day."

Antony maintained a dazed silence. Only his lips moved, framing without power to utter the words "Slap or two! Smash a saucer! Tear up a hank'cher!" Mrs Hawke stole a swift glance at him, and continued.

"Besides, Antony, you'm a man. You've got the firmness, and that's what the maidens want – a stiddy hand to keep 'em in order. I've been too soft with 'em all along, and that's the truth – always giving way and smoothing things down.

I didn' ought to be so, I know that; but 'tis my nature. A wake woman, b'lieve – a wake, fullish, easy-going, do-leave-us-be-comfor'ble sort o' woman."

"And that's the sort I want!" Antony burst out, with a thump on the table. "I'm a quiet chap myself, and look for a quiet home. I don't want none o' these saucer-smashers nor yet hank'cher tearers, nor I won't have none, and there's an end to it."

"Aw, Antony!" murmured Mrs Hawke. "'Tis so sudden. What will people say?"

"Don't care what people say," he declared, picking up his hat and buttoning up his coat. "Thanks be, I never asked either one the question, nor said a word they can bring up agin me."

"But Antony! To slight them for their own mother!"

"Hey!" The hat dropped from Antony's nerveless hand. Mrs Hawke gave him no time to recover himself, but flowed on.

"But if you don't care what people do think, then I don't nuther. There edn' a woman so wake but what she can stand up agin all the world if only she've got a man's strong arm round her.

"But aw, Antony dear, I never hoped 'twould come to this, not even when you said all those soft things to me just now, though I might ha' knowed you warn't the sort to deceive a poor trusting female. So if 'tis true as you do say, that I'm the sort you want, why then..."

She dropped her eyes, fingered her gown and whispered bashfully: "You can take me."

The numbness was already passing from Antony's brain. He saw before him an undeniably handsome woman, one who, by her own innocent confession, was at once soft-tempered, submissive and a compendium of all desirable accomplishments; one, moreover, who was obviously head over ears in love with him.

Was it necessary, or even expedient, to undeceive her, to inflict a cruel wound on that trusting heart? Nay, had he not been conscious from the very beginning of the inter-view of being drawn towards her by subtle spider-threads of elective affinity?

Was it not evident that by some lucky accident he had stumbled on that ideal mate for whom he had so long and vainly searched?

He looked across at her. There she sat, Love's plump cap-tive, with bowed head timidly awaiting his pleasure. He pulled himself together, laid hand on scissors and pen, and pushed them across the table.

"They'm yours by rights. Take them," he said with solemn tenderness. Mrs Hawke did not waste time in tak-ing them, but promptly melted into his arms.

So ended Antony's quest. I believe that the present Mrs Parkyn makes an excellent wife; though you who have read this story may think it a regrettable fact that the touch of vanity, from which not even the best of women is exempt, should in her case take the outward form of best boots two sizes too small.

But to what better use can a man's strong arm be put than to the support of a woman's tender, tottering footsteps

over the rough ways of life, as you may see Antony patiently doing every Sunday and holiday throughout the year?

This theme of a bachelor trying to decide between two sisters is a popular one for Lee. It is the subject of both his
one-act play The Banns of Marriage, and Mr Sampson.

PENHALIGON AND GALATEA

———◦•◦•◦———

THE ARTIST colonies of Cornwall are pleasant places to idle in, but to a man of my temperament the social distractions are too many to permit the production of decent work.

So when I heard that Gregson was going back to town for good, I arranged to take over his place, furniture and all. Gregson's place was a small cottage with studio annexed, situated in an out-of-the-way valley, quite twelve miles from an easel. There wasn't even a village near; the neighbours were scattered about in isolated farms and cottages, set out of one another's sight in the folds and turns of the valley.

The place suited me exactly. Engaging a woman to come up daily and see to the cooking and tidying, I settled steadily to work, undisturbed by art-chatter and musical evenings and the rest of the nonsense.

Of course I couldn't do without society altogether, but if the stranger knows how to conduct himself with decency and respect he will never lack entertaining company in the Duchy. "Bumpkin" is the last word to apply to the Cornish rustic, with his courteous manners, his alert Celtic wit, and his shrewdly humourous outlook on life. And if you have a collector's eye for the oddities of human character, you will find no better hunting ground than this land of solitary communities, where every house is a law to itself, and personal idiosyncrasies have ample elbow-room to flourish in. Our valley was as rich in eccentric types as a freak museum, and I had some queer experiences in my intercourse with them. Perhaps that affair of Mr Penhaligon was the queerest of all.

Mr Penhaligon and I began our acquaintance over a sketch I was doing by the roadside as he passed one afternoon. He was so good as to criticise it favourably – "Very handsome and very plain" was his verdict – and afterwards he lingered, discoursing on art and the kindred theme of whitewashing (on which he spoke with professional authority), until it was time for me to pack up and move homewards. Our ways lay together, and when we reached my cottage I could not do less than take his delicate hint, and ask him in to see the studio.

Among the lumber Gregson left behind him was a life-size female lay-figure. I had no use for the thing, but I did not trouble to remove it, and there it remained in a corner just as he had left it, dressed as an old country woman in shawl and bonnet, and seated in one of those attitudes of rigid limpness that only a lay-figure can assume.

Mr Penhaligon did not notice it at first; when he did, it was with a start, a muttered apology, and a deferential pull at his forelock. I began showing him some drawings, but his mind was evidently on the figure. He was too polite to stare directly at it, but every few moments his eyes would creep furtively round and be suddenly withdrawn. At last he could contain himself no longer.

"Begging your pardon," he whispered, "but the old lady there – she haven' moved a finger since I come in. P'raps you ought to see if there's anything the matter with her."

I laughed and explained.

"My life!" he exclaimed. "And I've ben thinking all the while 'twas your mother down for a visit, and fancying whether she'd had a stroke! And 'tidn' but only a doll all the while! Well, well!"

To entertain him, I played the showman, putting the figure into various attitudes and explaining the mechanism of the joints.

"What wonders we do live among!" said he. "Now I reckon one like she 'ud cost a pretty penny to buy – idn' that so?"

I named a probable sum.

"No, 'tidn' cheap. But then she don't cost nothing for her keep, s'pose. And she wouldn' be liable to wear out her clothes. Deaf and dumb, too. And blind overplus!" he continued with rising enthusiasm. "An't many such females going around, more's the pity. Reckon, now, you'll be terrible attached to her?"

Not at all, I explained. I had taken her over with the rest of the furniture, but she was quite useless to me, and in fact I should be glad to get rid of her.

"Sure 'nough?" said Mr Penhaligon, and fell into a deep fit of musing, his chin on his hand, his eyes fixed on the figure. Suddenly he turned round upon me.

"S'posing now," he said, "somebody should offer to take her off your hands, what would 'e be asking for her?"

I hadn't given the matter a thought, and couldn't say.

"S'posing now, somebody, like it might be myself, should offer 'e ten shilling for her, would 'e be willing to part with her?"

"Possibly," I said. "But whatever use – ?"

"Never mind 'bout that. I'll give 'e ten shilling for her. Come now!"

"You shall have her for nothing," I replied, "if you'll tell me what you want her for."

He eyed me doubtfully. "You do mean that?" he said. "And you won't go laughing upon me if I tell 'e? Well then – look-see. I'm a widow-man – wife been dead a twelve-month – and I live all alone. And there's more 'n one detached female hereabouts that think I didn' ought to live alone, and they ben't back'ard in hinting of the same. Don't say but what they'm right; 'tis terrible lonely up my way of a' evening. But I don't fancy none o' they.

"Now when you were showing off this, this person just now, it come into my mind of a sudden that here's the very one I'm looking for. She can't talk, that's true, but I don't want that – had twenty year of it and no stop already. Nor she can't work, but I don't want that nuther. You see, my wife that's gone, she lost the use of her limbs, barring her tongue, two year 'fore die, and I've got into my own way of doing things about the house, and don't wish no change. What I do want is somebody to sit over agin me 'front o' the fire of a' evening, with some knitting in her lap, or p'raps a penny story-book – somebody I can address a observation to now and agin, and not get my head snapped off for my pains. Or if I should have a drop at the inn, to come home and find somebody sitting up for me that won't call me a great guzzling toad. And somebody that'll keep the other females off, p'raps, though I wouldn' swear to anything short of a lawful wife doing that. Now she – come to think of it, she haven' got no name to her, s'pose?"

I succumbed to an irresistible temptation. "Galatea," I said.

"And a very good name too," said Mr Penhaligon, "though I don't mind hearing it before. Gal-a-te-a – rolls off the tongue like treacle, and plenty of it. My wife that's dead was Jane, short and sharp; if you wanted to vex her, call her Jinny. Ess, Galatea; and no objection to Gally for short; very nice and comfortable. She's the one for me. So thank 'e kindly, and I'll bring the dunkey and cart up tomorrow and fetch her home. But look – her face is a bit gashly, like you couldn' titch her up with a mussel o'red paint, now, could 'e?"

I readily promised to do this, and after thanking me again he took his leave.

When he arrived next evening, he had shaved his chin and smartened his clothes, and he carried in his hand a bulky bundle, done up in a shawl.

"You didn' say nothing 'bout the clothes," he explained, seeing my eyes on the bundle.

"So I've brought some of Jane's. I sized her up yes'day, and I reckon they'll fit very well, though I ben' sure 'bout the boots.

"The foot's much of a measure, I think, but Jane always

would have 'em two sizes too small, which didn' improve her temper. Same as those painting-tubes of yourn – squeeze one end, and 'tother's bound to bust out. Ah, you've coloured her up fine; brave and healthy she's looking, sure 'nough. Now Jane, she was dreadful pale and wisht, and no wonder, living like she did on heavy cake and indigestion mixture most of the while – one agin the other, like. Bad for the temper agin; peaceful stomicks make happy homes. Well, now–"

He paused, glanced in turn at the bundle, at me, and at Galatea, hesitated, and said in a shy undertone: "If 'twouldn' be asking too much would 'e mind stepping outside for a minute till I shift her things?"

I offered to help him. "Thank e'," he said, "but I'd rather you didn'. Can manage very well myself; done it scores of times for Jane after she was laid up, and she calling me a clumsy bufflehead all the while, poor dear. Beside," – he sunk his voice still lower in a kind of confidential embarrassment – "I've got all the trumpery complete here, and – you being a young bachelor – I thought p'raps you'd feel – well, a bit bashful, like."

A reputation for modesty is not a thing to endanger lightly. I promptly effaced myself.

When Mr Penhaligon called me in again, Galatea was completely transformed. She was sitting in a company attitude, bolt upright, eyes front; she wore a stiff black silk dress, adorned down the front with no fewer than four gold brooches, one above another; her bonnet was of jet black, set off with a red rosette over each ear; and her hands, sedately crossed in her lap, were genteelly encased in grey silk gloves.

"Looks handsome, don't 'a?" said Mr Penhaligon with evident pride. "Clothes fit very well, I think, though I had to let out the stays a brave lot, and the boots are a bit tight, as I thought they'd be. Lucky thing she an't subjeck to corns. But what do 'e think? When I went to shift her bonnet, I didn' notice 'twas tied under her chin, and her head come clane off with it. Give me quite a turn, as you may guess. But I've been thinking 'a'll be handy when I want to wash her face. I can take her head outside and put en under the pump, you see, without disturbing the rest of her. Well, time to be getting home-along. Now then, Gally, my dear."

With infinite tenderness he lifted her in his arms and carried her out, with her chin resting affectionately on his shoulder. I had occasion to remain behind for a minute. When I followed I found him in the road, with Galatea still in his arms, face to face with an extremely small and remarkably plump donkey, whose forward-pointed ears, upcurled lip and twitching nostrils were eloquent of her suspicion and disgust. Mr Penhaligon was cautiously advancing step by step, and step by step the donkey was retreating before him.

"Come, Jinny my dear," he was saying. "I tell 'e agin, 'tidn' nothing but a doll. Can't 'e trust uncle's word, my pretty? A great big doll – nothing but that. Come, my handsome!"

But Jinny only shook her head incredulously, and continued to back down the road. Mr Penhaligon appealed to me.

"Would 'e mind holding her head for a minute? Reckon she's jealous, poor dear; or else she reco'nise the dress. She and Jane never did hit it off together, for all their names are the same. Scratch her nose a bit, will 'e? – so's to keep her mind off while I get the other up. These females!"

Partially appeased by my cautious fondling, Jinny consented to stand still while Galatea was hoisted into the cart and made comfortable with the shawl and some cushions. Mr Penhaligon then mounted beside her, put his arm round her waist to keep here steady, took the reins, and bade me let Jinny go.

Jinny at once twisted her head round, brought one lustrous scornful eye to bear for an instant on the couple behind her, gave a derisory kick of her heels and started off at full gallop. When I had a last sight of them before they turned the corner, Jinny had not relaxed her pace and was edging nearer and nearer to the ditch, Galatea was bumping and swaying perilously from side to side, while Mr Penhaligon, with both hands strenuously occupied and his hat on the point of falling off, appeared (as I guessed by the movements of his head) to be earnestly and ineffectually remonstrating with either lady in turn.

When next we met, which was about a week later, I asked how he had got home.

"Pretty and well," he replied. "Only upsot twice, and no damage done. Gally fell a-top of me both times, so light as a feather. Jane fell a-top of me once, same way; but Jane weighed eight score when in good health. Ess, got home all right.

"Met several people on the way, though, which I didn' wish. Didn' stop to answer no questions; but next day! – well, if you'd passed my house any time next day, you'd ha' thought there was a burying on. Half the parish there, I reckon, one time and another.

"And the talk! Such sick talk you never heard, p'tic'lar from the women. They couldn' have 'bused me more, not if it had been a live one I'd brought home, and no ring to her. 'Twas 'Shame upon 'e, Penhaligon!' from one, and 'Enough to make poor Jane turn in her grave,' from another, and 'Honest flesh and blood ben't good 'nough for 'e, s'pose, that you must go and take up with a vain painted sack a' sawdust'. 'Twas one of those detached females said that, as you may guess.

"But I don't care for their talk, and so I told 'em. 'Show me as good a one,' I said to them, 'as handsome in the face and as quiet with her tongue, and I'll marry her tomorrow'. And so I would. 'Tis grand, I can tell 'e! When I come home, there she is, sitting up in her silk dress, doing nothing, like a real lady. Off hat, light fire, put kettle on, telling her the news all the while and no interrupting with foolish questions, and no calling me everything but a man because I didn' notice what colour dress Mrs What's-her-name-agin had on when I met her in the lane. When supper's ready, I hitch her chair up to table and set down opposite. Two cups o' tay; when I've drunk mine, we change over and I drink hers. After supper, p'raps I should read the paper to her, picking out the bits the women do like – fash'nable clothes and horrid murders and all that.

"Then, come nine o'clock, I put a silk hank'cher over her face, and so goodnight and sweet repose, as they say. Jane used to snore like thunder and talk in her sleep beside. Aw, 'tis grand! All pretending, 'course; though half the time I forget 'tis pretending. And what's life, after all? Nothing but that – pretending and fancying and fighting shadders and playing with dolls – that's of it, b'lieve."

With this philosophical summary of human existence Mr Penhaligon nodded and moved away, and I saw no more of him for some time. It must have been six weeks later when, being out for a ramble, I struck an unfrequented by-road, and came to a solitary cottage and saw in the garden, mounting guard over the vegetables, a strange, yet familiar figure. Dressed in a man's ragged tail-coat and a scanty red underskirt, with a battered straw hat tilted over her face, with one arm stretched appealingly heavenwards and the other stuck akimbo in a pathetic assumption of lightheartedness – could this forlorn draggle-tail be the once respectable Galatea? I went to the garden gate to get a nearer view. The click of the latch evoked a warning "Hoi, there!" – and I saw Mr Penhaligon hurrying down the path.

"Oh, 'tis you!" he exclaimed as he approached. "Step inside, and welcome. Thought 'twas one of these plaguy boys, coming in to make a mock o' the poor soul there. S'pose you catched sight of her, and come to see what's up. Ess, 'tis Gally, right 'nough. Come and look you'll find her sadly changed."

We picked our way among the peas and gooseberries, and halted in front of the poor disreputable thing.

"Young man," said Mr Penhaligon solemnly, "let what I'm going to show 'e be a warning for 'e not to give way to the drink."

With a dramatic gesture he whipped the hat from her head and revealed a great wound in her papier-mâché skull – a dreadful jagged hole that swallowed up half her forehead and the whole of one eye.

"Looks gashly, don't a?" he said. "Ugh! I can't bear to look upon 'urn." He clapped the hat on again. "Twas my own hand too that done the deed. Went down to the inn last Sat'day week. Gen'rally have a drop Sat'days, couple of quarts don't hurt nobody, and that's my 'llowance. But there was a passel of young chaps in there that thought 'twould be a fine joke to make the old man drunk, more shame to they. You know the way of it, I dare say. 'Jine me in a friendly glass, Penhaligon,' says one. 'You haven' had one with me yet,' says another. 'One li'll drop more won't hurt 'e,' says another agin. And then they begun to joke me about Gally here, and what with the drink and their tejousness, I got reg'lar fightable, come closing time.

"Don't mind how I got home. Come into the kitchen, struck a light, and there was Gally setting quiet by the fire, same as I'd left her. So I pitched telling her all the mockery I'd been suffering 'pon her account; and all the while she's goggling upon me, cold and scornful, like, till I begun to get mad. 'Spake up, will 'e?' I said. 'Call me a drunken blaggard if you've a mind to, so long as you say something.' No spake, of course, poor thing. 'Sulky toad!' said I. 'Spake up to once, or I'll make 'e yowl in good arnest.' No mouth-

83

speech, and eyes stark upon me all the while, like I was a worm, till I couldn' stand it no longer. Snatched up the poker and whacked to en. 'That'll larn 'e to stare,' I said, and went up over stairs to bed.

"When I come down sober next morning, there was the poor dumb crater crumped up in the chair with that terrible great hole in her head. I leave 'e to guess how I felt; 'tis a mercy I didn' go straight off and sign the pledge to once. Aw me, poor Gally!"

He sighed and lost himself in sorrowful meditation.

"But how came you to make use of her like this?" I asked. "I should have thought, valuing her as you did – "

"Now I ask 'e," he interrupted, "what would you have done in my place? I couldn' keep her on in the house. If you'd murdered somebody yourself, you wouldn' care about taking tay with the corp'. Nor I couldn' very well give her Christian burial. As for burning her on a bonfire, I hadn' the heart to do it, after the pleasant evenings we'd spent together.

"So there she was, and I didn' know what to do by her, till it come into my mind what a stately scarecrow she'd make. Bit of a come-down, I allow, after what she've been used to; but how's she to know that? And there an't a more capable scarecrow in the parish – I will say that for her. The blackbirds are took in complete by her, and even the sparrers don't care to come too close.

"And Jinny – you mind Jinny? Used to take me all my time to keep Jinny out of the garden. Gate shut wouldn' stop her; she'd lift the latch with her nose, walk in, and help herself to the cabbages. But you know what a dislike she took to Gally, first go-off; and now she won't set hoof inside the gate 'pon no consideration. Sometimes she'll stick her head over the fence and hoot, like she was mocking the poor dear, but that's as near as she'll come to her.

"So 'tidn' so bad, you see. Loss and gain – that's the way o' life, b'lieve. I do miss her comp'ny terrible, but the veg-e'bles are glad of it, I reckon. Come and see my broc'lo. You never set eyes on finer heads of broc'lo in your life, I'll be bound."

Believe me, it was in no spirit of mockery that I lifted my hat to Galatea as we moved away. She deserved a tribute of sympathy and respect, if ever a lay-figure did. Few of her race have endured such extreme viassitudes of fortune. I bared my head to her fallen grandeur, and wished her a long career of humble usefulness among the cabbages.

MARTHA AND THE BAILIFF

W HEN I was a youngster I used to go and stay
over to my uncle Antony's, holiday-time.
Uncle's boy Harry and me were just of an age,
and such a pair of young rogues you wouldn' find in all
Cornwall; there wasn' any kind of mischief but what we
were up to it, from tail-piping a dog to robbing an orchard.

Uncle had Tresolls Farm then, and a poor farm it was –
seventy acres up among the downs, and thirty of 'em
wouldn' grow nothing but furze and brambles. So when
grandf'er died and left uncle a bit of money, he began to
look about him for a better location.

Now just about that time old David Benney down to
Polgurney went smash at last, like everybody was looking
for him to do any time for ten year past. Polgurney was the
best-natured land in the parish – worth a fortune to a good
farmer, and David wasn' no bad one. But 'a wasn' worth
two fortunes to nobody; so David was sold up, and the
man that kept the inn slapped his pocket and said he'd
never hoped no better of poor old Dave. Uncle put in a bid
for Polgurney to once, and got en before the bailiffs were
out of the place.

Well, I was stopping up to Tresolls just then, and one
morning uncle told me and boy Harry to take the cart and
go down to Polgurney with a load of farm-stuff he wanted

moved to once. So we loaded up and went off, me and Harry and the dog. When we got there, 'twas getting up for twelve o'clock. Old Mrs Benney was outside in the garden, picking a bunch of flowers to carry away with her, for they were clearing out that evening. There wasn' much else for her to carry away, and she had to get permission, so she told us, before she could touch so much as a gilly flower.

"And aw, my dears!" says she, "if those vellans o' bailiffs haven' done my poor Martha to death before my very eyes, and she's in the crock this minute, boiling away for the rogues' dinner!" She was a great one for poultry, was Mrs Benney, and Martha was her favourite Cochin.

"Dear beauty!" says she. "And she'd ha' been safe and happy this minute, if 'a hadn' been for me and my temper. But I couldn' keep my patience with the nasty rogues, ordering me about in the kitchen where I'd been mistress for thirty year. So when one of 'em says: 'Fire's getting low, missus; get some coals, will 'ee?' I up and told him sharp to get 'em himself.

"How should I know poor Martha was in the cellar, try-ing to hatch out half a peek of best kitchen nobs? She always was a motherly soul, and if there wasn' no eggs handy, she'd set to 'most anything, so long as 'twas hard and roundish. I'd missed her yes'day, and I might ha' knowed – I might ha' knowed!" says the old lady, with the tears a-coo'sing down her cheeks.

"And presently," says she, "I hear a clocking and a flop-ping, and a voice saying: 'Warming the coals, are 'e? 'Tother way about, I reckon. Coals are going to warm you direckly.' And out come the murdering vellan, with Martha under his arm. 'Not that one!' I screeched. 'Take your pick – stags and hens, Wyandottes and Plymouth Rocks, but not Martha! She's terrible old and tough,' said I; and the Lord forgi'e me for slandering the poor dear beauty! 'All the better,' says he. 'I like something solid to chaw to. Twist her neck, Bill, while I see to the fire,' says he.

"And twist en 'a did before my face, and hadn' the dacency to go into the yard to do the deed. And then he said, 'Pluck her for us, missus,' he said, 'and you can join us when she's done.' 'Pluck her yourselves!' I said – for I was properly mad, I was – 'pluck her yourselves and eat her yourselves, and a bone of her in aich of your throats!' And so I comed away, and they laughing behind me.

"Aw dear, that I should live to see the day!" says Mrs Benney, and pitched groaning something cruel.

Well, we told her not to take on so, and then, being youngsters, we didn' know what to say else. We stood there, feeling very uncomfor'able, and wanting to laugh after that; and then Harry winked to me, and we crept off easy.

"It do seem a shame," I said to Harry. "Tisn' her copin no longer, that's true; but tisn' theirs nother. Tell 'ee what," said I, "I've a mind to play these bailiffs a trick."

"How a trick?" says Harry.

"Wait a bit," I said. "We'll go inside first, and see how the land do lay."

So in we went, and found 'em sitting one each side of the fire, pipe in mouth, and eyes on the crock. The bailiff was old Solomon Kitto, a fat, grey-whiskery old chap; 'tother was a little black-natured man with pig-eyes and a long nose; and just as we come in he reached forth and lifted the cover of the crock and geeked in; with the nose of 'm working like a rat's.

"'Most done, I reckon," he said.

Solomon up with a fork and jabbed it in.

"'Most", he said, "but we'll give her another ten minutes. Mustn' hurry poor dear Martha," says he. "She an't so young as she was."

Then he look round and see Harry and me.

"Hullo!" he said. "What you two young rogues doing here?"

"Larning roguery, 'course," I said, and Solomon glimped upon me sideways and scratched his head, but 'a couldn' take it up. So the other chap had a try.

"Won't 'e stay and pick a bit with us, my fine fellers?" says he, grinning like a badger. "We'm just going to pitch dinner, and I'll lay you'm hungry enough to savour even our poor fare." And then he lift the cover agin, and Martha did smell handsome, sure enough. But I knowed he was only farcing, like; so I said: "No thank'e," I said. "What we do eat, we steal for ourselves." And the little black chap, he glimped sideways and scratched his head.

Well, I stayed there a bit, taking notice of this and that, till I could see just how the land lay. Then I told Harry to come on, and we went out and pitched unloading. Out came the little black chap too, like I hoped he would, and leaned over the gate, watching us.

When we'd finished, I said to Harry: "Harry", I said, "I'm going to deliver poor Martha from those two hungry limbs."

"No, sure!" says he. "How?" says he.

"Stratygem," I said. "Got any bacca 'pon 'e?"

"Plenty," says Harry, hauling out six inches of twist.

"Put en up agin for the time," I said. Then I stood up, shading my eyes with my hand, like there was something in the distance I couldn' make out.

"That's the second time," I said out loud. "Wonder what she's up to, prowling around up there."

"Who?" says Harry, and looked the same way. And so did the little black chap.

"Why, Mrs Benney," I said, "up back of the mowhay, with a big basket over her arm."

The little chap didn' want to hear no more; off he went like the wind, straight for the mowhay. Soon as he's round the corner, "Now," I said. "I'm going to fetch Martha. You stroll up in front and slock old Solomon out."

"How?" says Harry.

"With your six inches of twist," says I. "Didn' 'e notice? They'd got their pipes on, but they warn't smoking, nor there wasn' but a stale smell of bacca about. They've smoked their allowance – that's where 'tis; and if I know anything about Solomon, he's just dagging for a whiff. So you slock him out," said I, "while I see for Martha."

"Right," said Harry, and went up front while I crep' round the back and geeked in. There was Solomon just hovering round the crock with a fork.

"Done to a turn," he said. "Where's that Bill?"

Then he crossed over to the front door. Soon as he showed himself, Harry called out: "Like a pipe o' bacca mister?"

Solomon look round, see Harry dangling the six inches of twist, and out he go, like a trout after a worm. In I slip, off cover, fork into Martha, and under my coat with her. She didn' stay there. She hadn' been an hour over the fire for nothing, Martha hadn'.

"What's this, you young rogues?" said somebody behind me; and there was Annie Benney, David's youngest maid, laughing all over her face.

"Apron, quick!" said I.

"You'll come to a bad end," said she, undoing the strings.

"So won't Martha," said I, snatching the apron and rolling the poor dear beauty up in it.

"Front door, then," said Annie. "I can hear 'em coming round behind."

Front door it was, and I catched Harry up by the gate.

"I've got her!" I said.

"No!" he said.

"Ess," I said. "And mind you drive slow till we've turned the corner, so's we shan't raise no unjust suspicions."

Into the cart all three, and slow it was to the corner.

"Now, thrash to en," said I. "Solomon's just about sarching the crock."

And off went the old mare like lightning, half a mile or so. Then we slowed up. Down we sit face to face in the cart, apron spread out for a table-cloth, and Martha smoking away in the middle. No knives and forks; but Solomon was right – she was done to a turn, and when we pulled to her legs she came to pieces in our hands. And there was the old greyhound joggling along with his nose to the backboard, snapping the bones so fast as we throwed 'em out, and covering up our tracks, like. Time we got home, there wasn' no Martha; she'd clane vanished off the face of the earth.

When we come in, there was the fam'ly setting down to dinner.

"Just in time, my dears," said Aunt Jane, "and brave and hungry you must be. Come along," says she, spooning out a couple o' platefuls of beef and taties.

So Harry looked 'pon me, and I looked 'pon Harry, and we shaked our heads, sorrowful-like.

"Don't know how 'tis mother," says I, "but I an't feeling a bit hungry this morning."

"Nor I nother," says Harry. "Tisn' what you may call hungry weather." Down tumble the spoon in the dish.

"My dear nerves!" said Aunt Jane. "What's up with the boys?"

"Aw, nothing," says Harry. "Only I don't fancy nothing just now, without 'tis a dish o' wake tay and a thin slice o' bread and butter."

"Wake tay and thin slice'll do very well here," I said.

"Tell 'e what 'tis," said Harry. "To my mind there's too much eating goes on. 'Tis bad for the health."

"Don't do to overload your stomick," said I, "partic'lar when you'm working hard."

Aunt Jane stood glazing upon us for a minute. Then she went to the cupboard and fetched a bottle. When Harry see that bottle, he begun to dodge round to the door. But Aunt got there first.

"This nonsense have got to be cleared out," says she. "If

you'm real bad, there's nothing like black draught; if 'tis nothing but mischief, it's as good as the stick. Anyways, you got to drink en before you set foot outside this room." And, aw, my dear life! – drink en we had to, sure enough.

"And now," said Aunty Jane, "father want 'e to take another load down to Polgurney, and make haste about it."

"Black draught and the stick!" says Harry when we got out. "Martha's coming expensive."

"Maybe 'tis all right, " I said. "Anyhow we got to chance it, so come along."

So we load up, and down we go agin. Down by the farm gate, there was old Solomon, looking so black as thunder.

"Now we'm in for it," said I. But you never know your luck.

"Hullo, you boys!" says Solomon. "Here's a purty job! If that old mother Benney haven' been and stole the fowl out o' the pot when my back was turned! Properly done us, sure 'nough, and me a bailiff of twenty years standing. But I'll pay her, see if I don't," says he.

"I was going to leave her carry away a side o' bacon, but not a rasher shall she have, the greedy old faggot! But that an't the worst of it," says he. "We might ha' made shift with the broth and some bread; but that fool of a Bill – aw, that fool of a Bill! – if he haven' been and heaved away all the broth, sarching for the fowl!"

'Bout a month afterwards we met Solomon agin. He stopped and looked us up and down, first one, then the other.

"You young blaggards!" he said. "You – young – blag-gards!"

— As told by Jacob Hoskyn of Port Oliver

Mrs Tonkin at Home

THE POSITION of Mrs Tonkin's residence and the arrangement of her kitchen windows are the envy of all her acquaintance. The principal window, which in most cottages would be the only one, merely looks across the narrow street to the yellow walls, mossy slate roofs, and doors and windows of the opposite houses, and is, besides, so crowded with geraniums and primulas that it is of little use, save for the minor and unimportant purpose of admitting light.

But the house being the corner house of a row, and situated on the verge of a kind of square or place (known as the Green, but innocent of verdure), the ingenious builder has seized the opportunity of inserting in the side wall, on a line with the fireplace, a subsidiary window, tall and narrow in shape, which not only commands a full view of the said Green – a favourite lounging and gossiping place – but rakes the main street of the village fore and aft, so to speak, for twenty or thirty yards, besides permitting a fairly comprehensive view of the harbour below.

The advantages this window confers are as obvious as they are enviable. Consider for a moment the unfortunate case of Mrs Matthews next door, or of Mrs Harvey over the way. Possessing windows of the ordinary kind, their outlook is so limited that scarcely has the passer-by come within range of observation than he, or she – which is more important – is hidden again, often before the poor ladies have had time to look up from their work.

At the best they are rewarded with the briefest, most tantalising of glimpses, and twenty times a day they must either interrupt their occupations to make a hurried rush for the street door, or leave their curiosity unsatisfied, and run a terrible risk of missing some interesting paragraph in the daily history of the town.

But with Mrs Tonkin it is otherwise. Every living creature that passes up or down the street comes under the scope of her observation for something like half a minute – time enough for the experienced eye to master every detail of dress and appearance, and to draw therefrom infallible deductions as to the victim's private affairs. A new ribbon at a maiden's throat, the neck of a bottle protruding from an old woman's gown pocket, the ragged sleeves of a married woman's jersey – such things speak volumes to the discerning mind.

Without leaving her "churrs", Mrs Tonkin can tell you who is prospering and who is not, who in love, who at odds with his wife, who is to have beef for dinner and who contents himself with salt fish. In short Mrs Tonkin is a happy woman, and all because of the little window.

The kitchen itself is a roomy apartment, floored with alternate squares of red and yellow brick, ceiled with bare varnished boards, and furnished, as to chairs and tables, in a fashion which calls for no remark. On the walls hang a few coloured almanacs and oleograph, and a large and

visit Cornwall to see – full ten feet high, with a thick woody stem, and bearing every year some hundred clusters of pink blossom. The loft communicates with the street by means of a dark passage or tunnel running down the side of the house farthest from the kitchen. This is the mode of ingress and egress of which the world mostly avails itself – the front door being reserved for gentry, beggars and "foreigners" generally.

<hr />

Now one winter afternoon Mrs Tonkin was in the kitchen beating – mending nets, that is – while her friendly lodger sat by the fireside keeping her company and filling the netting needles with twine as she required them.

The men – Peter the father, and Jimmy the son – lately home from the sea, were in the loft, mending the belly of the Petrel's trawl. Outside, on the Green, and by the railings of the harbour wall, some twenty or thirty fishermen were idling. Some leaned over the low railings, doubled up into impossible postures, the rest were performing a manoeuvre curious to behold.

They were in little groups of five or six, huddled together confusedly, chin on shoulder, as men might stand in a crowd. But instead of standing still, they were walking up and down with little short steps, four or five paces each way, jostling, shuffling, treading on one another's he every time they turned.

Sometimes he who held the ear of a group would reach an impressible point in his argument at the critical moment, and then, instead of turning with the rest, he would walk backwards in front of them, fugleman-wise, gazing earnestly into their faces and beating his palm with an emphatic finger.

Now and then a market-cart came clattering along the street at break-neck speed, the driver standing with legs wide apart (your Cornish Jehu disdains to sit), and then the conferences were seen to break up, and the groups scatter wildly, while mothers rushed screaming from their doors and snatched unconscious infants from the brink of destruction and a chorus of objurgations from all sides pursued the retreating vehicle.

Over the harbour wall there was a glimpse of the still blue pool, and the boats riding in it, drawn up in long parallel lines. Beyond that again was the open bay, flecked with white by the north-easter, and the great flapping brown sails of Devonshire trawlers lying at anchor off the harbour mouth. Now and then a jackdaw flew from his post among the chimneys and hovered over a heap of offal in a corner. Pied wagtails fought and chippered along the roofs and gulls traced complicated curves and reticulations against the sky.

It was market day, and a continuous stream of womankind – young, in gay hats and dressed, approximating more or less to the latest fashions, old, in bonnets and gowns of more sober stuff and cut – flowed past the window, bound for an afternoon and evening of mingled business and pleasure in the streets of the neighbouring town. Mrs Tonkin was in her element. She had fastened her net by a loop to a nail in the frame of the little window afore-mentioned, so that she could observe and comment at her ease without hindrance to her work. With her fingers busy about the net, she kept an easy flow of commingled criti-cism, anecdote and moral reflection, while the lodger lis-tened and wondered.

"There's Patience Ann James gwine to market in her shawl, athout a bonnet, ef I'd live! Well I sh'd be 'sha-amed! Sarah Tregurtha – a hard woman – d' keep a shop out 'long – d' gie long credit, and then, when you're as bar o' money as a toad is o' feathers, 'tes 'down wi' your cash' wi' she, 'or the law shall make 'ee'.

"They do say there's ill wishes flyen about Sarah's ears. I wouldn' be she, not for a thousand pound and a satin gown. Better a blow downright 'an a wish 'at d'come like a thief in the night, and you can't tell how nor when.

"Look at poor Martha Trier, lives down to quay. They do say Job Trier, aford 'a marry Martha, when courten anoth-er maid, and they fell out, and Job wouldn' ha' nawthen to do wi' she, but marr'd Martha, being his cousin. So the other maid wished agen Martha – wished her all manner o' things. And Martha's two sons were born big-headed (wit-less) and big-headed they've growed up."

The lodger, though not unaccustomed to hear similar tales, found this one too much for him, with its ghastly inference. He ventured to protest.

"Well, 'at's what they d' say," Mrs Tonkin replied with her usual cautious formula in reference to things supernatural.

"At's what they d'say, and 'at's what Martha herself d' b'lieve, and she's tauld me often."

"I wonder she doesn't retaliate," said the lodger.

"Plaize?"

"Hasn't she tried to pay the woman back in her own coin?"

"I don't doubt et. I don't doubt she's done her best, poor dear, but 'a be a poor wake crater – couldn' for the life of 'en wish agen a soul strong 'nough to raise a wart on the finger of 'en. Poor soul, when her second was born, and the doctor tauld her 'twould surely be like the first, a' wouldn' b'lieve en. "No" Martha'd say, "the Lord wouldn' let her" – manen the other one – "a wouldn' let her go so fur, I'm sure 'a wouldn', nor he wouldn' be so hard on me as to wish et." And she did go about for a long time, tellen us o' the clever things the poor chield did, and how 'a was sure the wits of en was sprouten – ay, 'twas a long time afore she give up hope, poor dear beauty!

"Eh-h! There's them maids o' Long Sam's in new gowns, as smart as paycocks, gwine out to catch the chaps. That's along o' Sam's luck wi' the fish this winter. There'll be a thousand herring on aich o' them maids' backs, I've no doubt.

"There d' go young Jimmy Green, whistlen. Why, Peter!" – calling to her husband outside. "Peter, I say!"

"Well there, what es 'a?" came from behind the door.

"Wadn' Jimmy Green converted up chap'l last revival?"

"Ess, sure."

"Well, 'a 've just gone in 'long, whistlen like a heathen. Edn' backslidden, is he?"

"Now, ef that edn' just like the women!" exclaimed Mr Tonkin, thrusting a red face in at the door.

"They be'old the nose of a conger, and they cry 'Say-sar-pent!' to wance. A chap can't breathe in this town athout breaking half the commandments ef you hark to what the women d' say."

"Well, 'tes well known that when you're converted you mustn' sing songs nor whistle, as ef you were 'a ordinary Christian, so to spake," said Mrs Tonkin.

"Hauld tongue! The lad's all right. You d' knaw how 'tes. Your heart may put off ets evil and be chucked full o' holiness, long afore your lips do forget their wicked ways. Jimmy Green's thoughts edn' whistlen, you may be sure – only the mouth of 'en. So don't 'ee go taking away his char'cter."

So saying, Mr Tonkin disappeared abruptly.

"I edn'," said Mrs Tonkin. "I edn' – but 'a should be more careful. Ef 'a was whistlen athout manen et – and I don't say 'a wadn' – et mayn't be no harm to spake of, sim-minly, but 'tes a sign o' the weakness o' the flesh.

"There d' go young Benny Dick."

The lodger, though foreseeing that the witticism would be wasted on Mrs Tonkin, could not refrain from asking if Benny Dick was a married man.

"Ess, to be sure," she replied, "a married man, poor chap

– marr'd last year – marr'd a woman from auver Port'leven, thought to do a clever thing, the fullish crater.

"Down here, sir, we don't like our people to marr' out o' the town, and these folk are worse 'an most foreigners – a passel o' roguish red-haired Danes. 'Why ded 'ee marr' 'en?' said one to Benny. 'Why,' said Benny, 'I'll tell 'ee. You d' knaw,' said he, Port'leven folk do stutter, every man Jack of 'em (and that's so, you caan't hardly make out what they d' say).

"Well, I had to marr' somebody, and I wanted a peaceful home, and I thoft a wife with a 'pediment in her spache 'ud be just the thing. So I went and picked out the maid 'at stuttered worse o' the whole bunch.'

"Well, week after they were marr'd, Benny thought to try her. 'A waited till Sat'day come, and she'd claned the floor and then 'a come up from the boat with his say-boots on, all mud and muck and wet laaken, and 'a marched into the kitchen and stands there afore the fire as bauld as ye plaize. Presently she come down auver steers, and 'twas as good as a play to see her stand theer scaulden and profanen somethen dreadful, I've no doubt, inwardly, but not a word could she coax through her teeth.

"Benny, he laughed, thinken he's master now, sure 'nough, when down she falls in a fit. They runned for the doctor.

"Doctor took Benny aside. 'Take care how you d' anger your wife,' he said. 'You see, spache to a woman is like the hole in the top of a pot – lets off the steam when 'a do bile up. But stop the hole, and there's 'a accident. I waan't say more 'an this, et may be as bad as murder ef you d' anger your wife, so take care.'

"And ever sence then, the poor chap caan't call his soul his own."

Breaking off the report of Mrs Tonkin's discourse at this remarkable anecdote, a pause is made to explain that even the brief specimen just given was not without its interruptions. It is seldom indeed that the kitchen remains empty of visitors for ten minutes at a time – least of all on market day, when all the world is abroad.

Various reasons contribute to make it one of the chief places of resort in the village, ranking equal at least with the grocer's shop, the bakehouse and the "short" or well. Its central position has something to do with this. Then its mistress is generally popular, as a sensible, good tempered woman, with a large fund of available sympathy for friends in trouble, a good listener, a good talker and, above all, one of whom it has been said that no woman is easier to borrow from.

The habit of borrowing, like the kindred habit of running into debt, has a peculiar fascination for these folk, and in some cases it develops into a positive mania, its victims borrowing at all times and seasons, without necessity, and apparently from sheer delight in the act. They are reluctant to quit a neighbour's house without carrying off some spoil or other; if the frying pan they come to claim is in use, or has already been left, then a pinch of saffron, a spoonful of yeast, or last week's newspaper will serve their need just as well.

Several of them are in the habit of sponging regularly on Mrs Tonkin, coming daily, and seldom going empty away. She submits with great good humour, regarding it as a neighbourly duty, and merely contenting herself, when the raiders have departed, with shaking her head and remarking that "they that go a-borrowing go a-sorrowing".

Then she is reputed to spend less time than any living woman in "coozing" or gadding about on gossiping tours. Naturally, visitors are more frequent at a house where the mistress is actually as often to be found at home as not. Moreover when one of the newsmongers — and there are twenty dames in the village who benevolently give up their whole time to the business, resolutely sacrificing their own trivial household affairs to the good of the community — has a special bit of information to circulate (a death, a ghost, a pretty scandal or what not), she will not have been half an hour about it before she reflects: "There's that poor Mrs Tonkin, she never do g' out — s'ch a workish woman as 'a es, 'twill be a kindness to go tell her to wance."

Then, there is the fact that Mrs Tonkin is second cousin to at least half the village, and that every relation passing the door is by duty bound to look in and chat. If to relations, borrowers and newsmongers, you add her immediate neighbours who are in and out of the house all day, as well as people on business and casual visitors from other villages, you will begin to realise to what a formidable length a bare list of her daily callers would extend.

To chronicle in detail all the visits of the afternoon would be tedious – it will suffice to select two or three of the most remarkable as specimens, and pass over the rest in silence or the briefest mention.

———⟡———

One of the earliest visitors was Mrs Tonkin's next door neighbour and special crony, Mary Ann Matthews, a tall, grey-haired woman with a worn, sweet face and a soft, pleasing voice. She wore her shawl over a peaked cloth cap, and had her knitting in her hands.

The two women exchanged greetings in the peculiar recitative which is used in salutation and in question and answer, and gives the most commonplace talk the charm of music. In fact, it is a musical phrase, sung rather than spoken, beginning on a low note, rising a fifth to the emphatic word, and then dropping by semitones.

"Well my dear, 'edn' gwine market then?"

"No, Mrs Tonkin, my dear. Maister's just come home from Plymouth. You edn' gwine neither?"

"No. Must finish this plaguy old net ef I d' live. What ded 'ee fit for denner today, Mrs Matthews?"

"Oh, just cabb'ge soup and ling and teddies. What was yours?"

"Oh hadn' time to fit nawthen proper. Us just had

106

Sat'day's denner – catch 'em and take 'em, as they d' say – a bit here and a bit there. So John Matthews is back?"

"Ess, 'a b'lieve – come back this morning."

"Any luck wi' the fish?"

"No. Not a herring all the while – terr'ble bad luck. 'A should ha' come back full three weeks ago, but you d' knaw how tes, crew say 'Let's stop on a bit longer – maybe the luck 'll turn' and so they stop and run the debts up till salesman waan't lend another farthing, and back they come worse off 'an they did start. Poor John. I knawed how 'twas, minute I set eyes on 'm. Wet laaken and tumblen tired 'a was, and 'a never said a word, but just dropped in a cheer and sat.

"And little Annie, she runned up and jumped on his knee, and said 'What's brought home for ma and me, da?' – for 'a mostly gets a dolly or a mug up Plymouth for 'en. And John he looked up and stroked her hair, and said, 'Just a fine cargo o' torn nets and twenty pound worth o' debts, my dear. Edn' that brave?' said he. Well, I wadn' what you call joyful, you may be sure, but with he that bitter 'twouldn' never do for me to gie in, so said I, 'Never mind, Annie, my dear, da's brought hisself home safe and sound, so us waan't mind the nets, nor yet the debts,' said I."

"Sure, right 'nough!" said Mrs Tonkin, with a world of sympathy in her voice. "Nets nor yet debts," she repeated approving sentiment and jingle alike. "Tes queer how the luck do run. Et do come and go like wind and tide. Some do swim in 't – some don't never get a taste of 't."

"John did try to get Lucky Harry on our boat last season," said Mrs Matthews, "offered 'en haalf captain's share if 'a would come, but 'a said no – said 'a wouldn' sail with a captain whose hair was red – doubted ef his luck'd hauld in that case. And I'm sure my John edn' what you may call red-haired azackly – yally, I caall'n."

"You're right my dear," said Mrs Tonkin with conviction, "yally 'a es – just the colour of oranges, and that's a lovely colour. But as for Lucky Harry, I wouldn' ha' nawthen to do wi' en, ef I was cap'n. Luck like his edn' nat'ral – not in a great rogue like he. I d' want to knaw where et do come from and what price 'a do pay for 't."

"Well," said Mrs Matthews, lowering her voice, "they do say somethen about a great tall man in black, people see round Harry's door after dark. But 'tes all nonsense, 'a b'lieve," she added, glancing towards the lodger.

"So 'a es, my dear," assented Mrs Tonkin reassuringly.

"But I waan't never have 'en on my boat. 'Tes well known how they that d' 'ave 'en do pay for 't after. Running after luck edn' the way to catch 'en. Look at Betty Trevean. Ef any woman could be lucky by trying, 't would be she. Why, 'twas only last week she comed in here and axed to borry my bottle o' giant cement I use to mendie dishes and cups wi'. 'What have 'ee scat, Betty?' said I. 'Edn scat nawthen,' said she. 'Then wherefore com'st thou a-bor-ryen?' said I. I'll tell 'ee said she. 'When I come down this mornen,' said Betty, 'I found a snail on my windy.' 'At's a good thing,' said I – thinken upon the saying – 'The house is blessed, where snail do rest.'

'Ess, a good thing,' said Betty, 'ef 'twill only stay here.

But I only had one wance afore,' said she, 'and then 'a dedn' stop time 'nough to let the luck soak in, so to spake. Now,' said Betty to me, 'I was thinken this time I'd make my luck sartin sure, so I'm gwine to take this here cement, and cement the baste down to the windy glass. Crater's as well theer as anywheres,' said she. 'Tes for et's own good and mine too.'

'Mind what you're a-doen of,' said I. 'Tes the first time I've heerd tell o' making your luck stick wi' cement, and I don't think 'twill serve,' said I."

"And sure 'nough," concluded Mrs Tonkin impressively, "that very night the cat got into Betty Trevean's spence, broke three dishes, and ate up Betty's Sunday mate."

<hr />

Here the door swung open and Mr Tonkin entered from the loft, bringing with him a strong odour of Stockholm tar. Keeping his eyes fixed on an imaginary point some miles off through the wall, he rolled across the room with the true fisherman's gait – which is the sailor's gait differentiated into lumpishness by constant wearing of heavy sea boots – and brought to, six inches from the bars of the grate. With his arrival Mrs Tonkin put off her humanity and became a wife.

"Hullo!" she exclaimed sharply. "You edn' finished mending that trawl, I'm sure. Go back to thy work, thou sluggard, go!"

"Can't a chap never have a touch pipe for a bit in this house?" was Mr Tonkin's plaintive query.

"Touch pipe indeed! Simmin to me, you don't never do nawthen else."

"These women!" said Mr Tonkin, turning to the lodger. "They're a puzzle! Caan't liv a man be and let 'n do his work in his own way at his own season!"

"Work!" from Mrs Tonkin in white-hot scorn.

"Ess work! What do the women know o' work. What's your work to ours? I'd like to see a crew o' women draw a net on a bad night. A hard life sir, we d' 'ave and our wives do their best to make et harder."

"Tcha!!" exclaimed his wife, whose contempt had passed beyond the stage when it could be expressed in words.

Mr Tonkin, who rather prides himself on his eloquence, now drew himself up and embarked on an oratorical effort.

"Ess – a hard life, and a poor trade – the meanest trade there is. Our toil's that bitter, et do take the sweetness out o' the bread we earn thereby. We d' 'ave wind and say for mates, and they're like beasts in a cage, and lie and wait for a chance to turn and wreck us, as the sayen is. Ess, we do snatch every morsel of our bread out o' the jaws of death, 'a b'lieve. I tell 'ee, sir, I've lived on the say and by the say, all my life, but I hate the sight of 't and I hate the sound of 't. Ef I could go inland, that's where I'd like to live, sir – 'mong the trees, where nawthen 'ud meet my sight but trees and green herbs. Out o' sight and hearing o' the say for ever and ever – that's where I'd like to be."

Mr Tonkin's rhetoric, though rude, was really quite

impressive, the lodger thought, all the more so for its broken delivery. But it had no effect on his wife.

"Well," she said, "I like to taste the salt in the air I d' breathe, same as in the vittles I d' ate. And I don't think much o' people 'at grummle over the way their bread and butter's cut, when they've cut 't themselves."

"Oh you!" said Mr Tonkin, paying back an instalment of score. "Come, edn' 'ee gwine to fix a dish o' tay?"

"Tay!" returned his wife. "Tay! Ess, 'tes allers tay wi' you. Drink and grummle – 'at's all you men be fit for – grummle and drink tay. And to hear 'ee talk about your toil and your hard life! Why edn' 'ee on the say now, arning a liven? Awe ess! We d' knaw what the auld woman said for the men o' this town! When there's calm they cussn't goo, an' when there's wind they wussn't goo."

After this sarcasm, which every fisherman in the village is fated to hear at least once a day when on shore, Mrs Tonkin, whose treatment of her husband embodies no real ill-feeling and must be regarded as part of her scheme of conjugal duty, relented so far as to add, "Well, shalt have thy tay, a poor dear, go, take the jug and g' out for a cuse o' water, and tell Jimmy to bring a stog o' wood and some coals for the fire."

But though he had gained his point, Mr Tonkin still lingered. The shifting of his feet showed that he had something on his mind. He gazed steadily out of the window.

"Come, bustle," admonished his wife.

Mr Tonkin cleared his throat nervously.

"I've used the last o' my baccy," he said in even tones,

carefully expressive of indifference to the import of his statement.

"You d' smoke all day. Ef you c'd smokie and sleepie too, you'd smokie all night!" was Mrs Tonkin's comment. "Go, take up the jug and bustle."

"Come Ann, gie us the money," he burst out desperately.

"Money? What money's that?" in well-simulated astonishment.

"For some baccy – there's a good soul."

"I'll gie 'ee the stick rather!" – in a tone of great ferocity. "Two shillen a week, Mrs Matthews, they d' cost me, and nawthen but stinking smoke to show for 't. Go, do what I tell 'ee, go!"

"I'll go trust Mrs Maddern for a' ounce, then," threatened Mr Tonkin.

"Mrs Maddern d' knaw better 'an to let 'ee have et, I reckon. There edn' a wife in this town haven't warned Mrs Maddern agen letten their men trust her. She d' knaw who hold the purses 'a b'lieve."

"Then I'll go borry'n off o' somebody," declared Mr Tonkin, playing his last card.

"Ess, go disgrace yourself and me too! Go begging for a haapord o' plug, like a shiftless laverack of a longshoreman! No, we edn' beggard yet," feeling in her gown for her pocket, "though that edn' no fault of yours. Go, take thy money, go."

Mr Tonkin received the money and rolled away, generously – or politically – omitting to express any triumph at his victory.

"Ah well!" said Mrs Tonkin, "tes a bit too bad to makie s'ch a fuss over thruppence, but that's the only way to trate 'em. Show yourself soft to a man, and 'Hullo' 'a says, 'ere's a brae fine cushion, and he up and dabs his great boots upon 'ee to wance. Hard as sparkles a wife should be, or she's a slave."

Mrs Matthews, who had politely affected obliviousness during the last few minutes, now recovered to say softly, "But when a man's in trouble, like my John."

"Don't 'ee make a mistake, my dear!" cried Mrs Tonkin vehemently. "Show yourself harder 'an ever. Scauld 'en, garm at 'en, stir 'en up, anger 'en, don't let 'en set still and ate his heart out. 'At's the way."

Evidently Mrs Matthews did not believe in such drastic treatment, but not being a woman of argument, she only smiled sadly and shook her head.

"What wi' Peter and Jimmy, I ought to knaw what men are like," added Mrs Tonkin, "and I don't stand no non-sense from they, you may b'lieve."

<hr />

As she spoke, Jimmy Tonkin entered with the firing. Having disposed of his load, he did as his father had done a minute ago – went to the window and gazed out, shifting his feet and clearing his throat uneasily meanwhile. Seeing his pipe in his hand, the lodger guessed what was coming, and awaited the issue with curiosity.

Jimmy has a handsome face, and a wheedling tongue, and disdains his father's coarser methods on such occasions as this. He began the attack with a little judicious flattery.

"How's the net gett'n on?" he said.

"Why 'tes 'most finished, ef I d' live!"

"Wonderful quick you be, and no mistake. I doubt ef there's another as quick."

"Well, I wadn' never 'counted slow, 'at's true," said his mother, with a laugh of flattered modesty. "But there's many as good, I've no doubt."

"I never seed 'en then," replied Jimmy. "Da gone for a cuse o' water?"

"Ess. Gone to Mrs Madder's for his baccy too, 'a b'lieve?"

"Ha, ess. So you give 'en the money, did 'ee? Said 'a was gwine to ax 'ee for 'nt. Said to me, 'Jimmy, you're out o' baccy too'. 'Ess,' said I. 'Then I'll tell the missus to gie me enough for both,' said he. 'No,' said I, 'when I do want 'n I'll ax for 'n. I've had two ounces this week,' said I, 'and that's as much as I should. Ma d' think et waste an' maybe she's right. I'll just jog on to Sat'day athout et.' 'Wait tell you see me smoken afore 'ee,' says father. 'There'll be envy in your heart, and wrath in your stummick,' 'a said to me, 'and you'll be ready to gie the world to touch pipe for a bit, that 'ee will,' 'a said. 'Maybe,' said I, 'but I edn' gwine to plague ma, ef 'tes only for thruppence. She d' 'ave plagues enough as 'tes,' said I."

The artful Jimmy made a feint of retiring to the loft.

"Here, stop a bit!" called his mother. "Ef your father d'

114

'ave his baccy, so shall you – 'at's only fair, 'a b'lieve. They shaan't say I show favour, or trate 'ee defferent."

"No, no," murmured Jimmy, with the air of a martyr, or a tempted saint. "I edn' gwine to take et."

"Take et to wance, I tell 'ee, and be off wi' 'ee," cried Mrs Tonkin in a pretended rage.

"A good lad, Jimmy, so 'a es," she added when he had gone. "A bit lazy, and a bit too p'tic'ler over his mate – but a good lad."

The lodger caught the eye of Mrs Matthews. She said nothing, but her wink was eloquent.

When, soon after, she had taken her departure murmuring something about "getting back to John and little Annie," a long legged nephew of Mrs Tonkin's slouched in, sat for five minutes in unbroken silence, and slouched out again. He was succeeded by a little, dirty-faced boy who asked if "plaize would Mrs Tonkin lend ma some sugar and a noggin o' paraffin and her best taypot, because ma had quality people from foreign parts coming to tay, and didn't want the town to be put to shame by a pot athout a spout" – an appeal to Mrs Tonkin's patriotism which had the desired effect.

A breathless dame thrust her head in at the door, screamed something – presumably a piece of news – in unintelligible Cornish, and vanished. Mr Tonkin and Jimmy returned, rolling in unison, and enveloped in triumphal clouds of smoke.

Mrs Harvey from over the way, having seen through the window Mrs Tonkin getting out her best teapot, came in under the impression that a meal was preparing. Being undeceived, she made a futile attempt to hide the hunch of bread she had brought to spread with Mrs Tonkin's butter and dip into Mrs Tonkin's pekoe, and departed hurriedly. Mrs Tonkin explained to the lodger that "Mrs Harvey never lifts her gown (pays money) for tay – what she do 'ave, she d' 'ave on the cheap. But she'd never be beholden for bread to a soul". A little proper pride sometimes goes a very long way.

———◦———

And so the afternoon wore on, and visitors came and went, until Mrs Tonkin, hearing a weighty footstep, which was yet not the clumping step of a man, resounding in the back passage, exclaimed, "That's my sister, Jane Polsue, for sure. Now there'll be some hollering and argufying, 'a b'lieve."

Mrs Polsue's shrill voice was heard exchanging bantering greetings with the men in the loft, and then in she waddled in her market-going array, bonneted, apronless, basket over arm, and upper part of her ample person rightly sheathed in a glossy jacket of imitation sealskin. By the time she had advanced to the middle of the room, it was discovered that she was not alone.

Clinging half-hidden among her skirts, and swinging to and fro with every movement of her body, was a little girl of six or seven, wonderfully arrayed in a crimson plush frock, a necklace of bright blue beads, pink stockings, and a white straw hat trimmed with green ribbons.

"Come out, my 'andsome, and show thyself!" exclaimed Mrs Polsue, extricating the child from the folds of her gown and pulling it forward.

"Theer, Ann, what d'ye think o' that? Edn' she fitty? Edn' she rale 'andsome – as smart as a guckoo-fish? She's Lizzy Ellen's little maid, and she's a-gwine wi' Aunt Jane to market – edn' 'ee, my dear?"

"Eth, 'a b'lieve," lisped the child.

"Eth, 'a b'lieve!" echoed Mrs Tonkin admiringly. "Hark to the minnam! 'Eth, 'a b'lieve,' she d' say, as formal as the Mount. Set down, my worm, while I get 'ee a cake."

"Well, Ann, and how many nets have 'ee done?" asked Mrs Polsue, as Mrs Tonkin returned from the cupboard with a generous slice of saffron cake.

"Well, I reckon this is the fourth this week," replied her sister with conscious pride.

"Fourth! You'm a reg'lar busker, Ann, and no mistake."

"Well, I do hate to be diddlen about doing nawthen."

"You might ha' found time to go to poor Dicky Trewarven's berrin' yes'day, though."

"Aw. You went, I s'pose, Jane?" said Mrs Tonkin.

"Ess, o'course. I haven' missed a berrin' in this town for twenty year – summer or winter, cauld or het, dry or wet – and there edn' many can say the same. 'Do unto others as you would that they sh'd do to you' – that's my motty, and I turn et this way, 'Go to other people's berrin's that they may come to yours'.

"Eh – 'twould be a wisht berrin, that!" chuckled Mrs Tonkin.

"You d' knaw my manen, Ann," said Mrs Polsue placidly. "But I wonder 'ee dedn' go."

"Me? Dicky wadn' no friend o' mine."

"All the more cause for 'ee to go to 's berrin'," said Mrs Polsue warmly. "Quarrels should end when your foe's in his box."

"Nor he wadn' no foe neither," said Mrs Tonkin.

"Well, then, you should ha' gone, ef 'twas only for the credit o' the town. I do hate to see a berrin' empty o' folk – not but what there was a brae pillow up to poor Dicky's. I did walk in front along o' Benny-Bath's-wife-Annie's-sister-from-foreign-don't-knaw-the-name-of-'en. And I tell 'ee Ann when we come to the rope-walk out 'long, and I look behind, and behold the percession, two and two, stretchen all the way back, most as fur 'a you c'd see, all in proper black, every mawther's chield of 'em, and then the box and six tall chaps a-carr'n of 'en, and then the fam'ly haulden their handkerchers – et fair made me shever.

"And says I, 'tes a pit a man caan't walk at his own berrin' – Dicky 'd be a proud wan this day, sure 'nough, to see what honour the world do hauld him in now he's deed. And we did sing Peace in the Valley as we did go – 'twas Dicky's favourite – and when 'a was on his bed 'a said for us to sing et, and sing et we did. That theer sister to Annie Bath have got a fair sweet voice, sweet as honey, but 'a put me out somethen terrible, for 'a would sing seconds – said they'd pitched the key so high she was afraid she'd scat her

118

voice up top ef a' should sing the tune. And you knaw how 'tes wi' me, I couldn't sing seconds wi' she, nor I couldn' keep tune wi' the rest, and theer I was, a-wandering about in a maze all the while atween the two. Ess my voice was a lost sheep that day, 'a b'lieve. Et put me mad, et did, and her a foreigner. 'Twas a trate to hear her, though."

"A sweet voice," said Mrs Tonkin the moralist, "is far above rubies, a possession athout price. Virtuous be'aviour waan't gie 'ee riches, but et–"

"Do 'ee talk sense, Ann," Mrs Polsue interrupted, "and don't prache, and listen to what I'm tellen 'ee. When the berrin' was over, I walked back wi' poor Dicky's aunt Blanche, and she tauld me all about the partic'lars of how he died.

"Three tokens there were, she did say. First was when a little maid come in to play wi' Dicky's young brothers, and she got drawing on a slate. 'Look, Dicky,' she said, 'what a pretty thing I've drawed.' Dicky looked. 'Why,' said he, going as white as a wall, 'tes a box – a coffin sure 'nough.' And so 'a was, and Dicky the first to name et. Then, on the day 'a was took bad, they come down in the morning and found Dicky's watch fallen off the nail on the wall, and the glass scat in pieces – manen, I s'pose, that time was to be o' no more account to him. And the laast token was when Dicky's little brother was setten alone in the kitchen ateing cake, and the door o' the loft opened wide and shut again, and when the lad runned out to see, there wadn' nobody there. 'Tes thought to sinnify the coming into the house what no mortal eye has seen."

Mrs Polsue paused for a moment. Then she continued.

"The poor chap was sensible nearly up to the laast. They axed him, 'You edn' afraid to die, Dicky?' 'No, no,' 'a said smiling, 'you d' knaw I settled all that laast November month' – manen when 'a was converted up to the revival.

"And near the end, setten theer, they heerd a 'thump, thump,' like a hammer somewhere in the chamber. 'What's that?' said one. Twas the heart of 'en beating. Blanche said et put them in mind ef 'twas his sperrit knocking to be let out. Just at the last 'a begun to wander, and thought 'a was a little lad again, and talked o' lessons and marbles and axed his mawther for ha'pennies. Et made their hearts sore to heark to 'n.

"Then he shut his eyes and they thought 'a was gone, but sudden 'a sat up and turned his head to listen, and, said he, 'Mother, there's Mally Rowe outside, a–caalling'. Mally, you d' knaw, was a little maid they used to caall his sweet-tard when a lad – been dead these ten year. 'Mother,' 'a said, 'there's Mally caalling. Ess, I've done my sums, and my spelling, and my lessons, every one, and I'm gwine out to play wi' Mally.' And then he falled back, and 'twas all over."

"Dear heart!" said Mrs Tonkin softly, and there was silence for a while.

"What ded Dicky die of?" asked Mrs Tonkin.

"Well," replied her sister, "he hadn't been what you may call rusky, not for a brae bit of a while. Just afore Christmas he went out cur'l singen, and catched a cauld – nawthen to speak of. So his mawther said, 'Just you stop indoors for a day, and I'll gie 'ee some moogwort, and you'll be right in a jiffy.' But no, 'a said 'twas nawthen, and 'a went traipsing about singen cur'ls wi' the lads and maids, up to three in the mornen. Then 'a was took bad, and they sent for the doctor. Information o' the lungs was what he called et."

"Which doctor was that?" asked Mrs Tonkin.

"Club doctor, to be sure, Doctor Vivian."

"Well, I don't think much o' he."

"You may well say that, Ann. Why, they axed 'en to gie Dicky some med'cine, but such stuff as 'a gave 'en! – a teeny little bottle, 'at dedn' hauld haalf a noggin – and said for 'em to gie 'n a tayspoonful twice a day. What good could that do 'en? Now ef they'd gone to Doctor Borlase, he'd ha' guv 'em a good quart o' stuff right off, I warrant – and brae 'm strong and nasty stuff too. But this here – why Blanche tasted 'n, and 'twas like raspberry serrup for flavour.

"No wonder the poor chap's gone, though his mawther did gie 'n a pint of moogwort every time wi' the other stuff to make up for 't. 'Ah,' he'd say for the moogwort, 'that's good, I can feel 'n all the way down, and taste 'n for haalf an hour'. But 'twadn' no manner o' use."

"A should ha' tried helder," said Mrs Tonkin. "What's moogwort? No bad tipple for a bit of a cauld, maybe, but et don't go to the stummick like helder. Nawthen beats helder to my thinken."

"Aw, ess, Ann – we'd all knaw you and your helder," replied Mrs Polsue with easy score.

"Tes all one to you – be it a toothache or be it a bad leg or be it the croup, out you come wi' your helder. Now ef you axed me, I sh'd say camm'ile to wance. 'Tes twice as infectious."

(Let no one accuse Mrs Polsue of ignorant maltreatment of the English language. All she has done is to take two synonyms – "efficacious" and "effective" – one of which is clearly superfluous, fuse them together, and give the result an appropriate medical flavour).

"Well, Jane," said Mrs Tonkin, with real emotion in her voice, "I wonder at 'ee I do. You d' knaw we were all brought up on helder. Mawther never gave us nawthen else. I waan't say camm'ile edn' good, nor I waan't say moogwort edn' good for they that's used to 'ut, but helder's our family med'cine, so to spake, and why don't 'ee stick to 'ut? Many's the noggin of et you've swallied, or you wouldn' be alife and rusky now, 'a b'lieve. And now to turn and score and 'buse et – 'tes downright fullish, Jane, and I wonder at 'ee."

"Wonder away, my beauty," said Mrs Polsue flippantly. "Long as you don't try to make me swally your wash, I don't care."

"Wash!" screamed Mrs Tonkin, and plainly a quarrel was imminent, when the little girl, who was kneeling on the window seat, looking down the street, began clapping her hands.

"Look, look!" she cried, "big man, thuch a big man!"

The ladies suspended their dispute, and getting into the line of sight from the window, began to bob their heads from side to side and crane their necks in an effort to get a fair view. The lodger had that morning seen a party of startled cormorants on a rock perform exactly the same antics.

"Tes long Jacob Penelloe and that chatterin' daughter o' his!" exclaimed Mrs Polsue. "What a size that man is! 'A come a'courten me once, Jacob did, but I wadn' gwine to marr' a chap whose face I couldn' slap athout getten on the table. Lucky I dedn' for ef I'd had that magpie Vassie Penelloe for daughter I'd ha' been drove mazed afore now. They edn' comen in here, I hope, Ann?"

"Ess, 'a b'lieve. Jacob's mother's sister marr'd our aunt Ellen Elizabeth ef you d' mind, and being a sort o' cousin, 'a mostly drops in when 'a d' come by."

"Then I'm off," declared Mrs Polsue. "Come Lizzy, my beauty."

"Wait in the loft for a bit, Jane," said Mrs Tonkin. "Being country folk they'll come to the front door, and ef you wait you won't meet 'em."

In fact, at that moment there was a rapping on the front door, and while Mrs Polsue retired at the back, Mrs Tonkin bustled out into the entry, and the sound of salutations was heard.

"Aw, ess, to be sure – plaized to be'old 'ee once more. Step inside, my dear, step inside, Mr Penelloe, and set down for a bit. Long legs d' want a rest, as much as short ones, 'a b'lieve."

Miss Penelloe enters – a plump, youngish woman,

ruddy, black-haired, with a typical Celtic face, high cheek-bones, small twinkling grey eyes, and a long upper lip like a portcullis over a big, thin mouth. Behind her stooped her father, immensely tall, thin, loose-jointed, near sighted and wearing a big grizzled beard.

Mrs Tonkin introduced the lodger. Miss Penelloe nodded and smiled graciously and remarked on the state of the weather, in an affable tone, calculated to set him at his ease at once. Mr Penelloe stood and swayed about in the middle of the room, gazing helplessly at the net, whose coils surrounded him on the floor. His daughter proceeded to take him in hand.

"Step auver the net and set down, father. Gie me your hat, or you'll be setten on 't – s'ch a habsent man as you be. Don't 'ee set theer in a draught, and you with a cold, come auver here," catching him by the elbow, and steering him to a chair in a corner where he collapsed limply.

"Ess, Mrs Tonkin," she continued, sitting down and folding her hands, "us couldn' pass your door and not look in for a bit of a chat. 'Tedn' often we d' come this way. And how's your health Mrs Tonkin?

"What are 'ee a-sarchen after father? Your pipe? Here 'a es, in my bag. No trusting father with his pipe, 'a b'lieve, Mrs Tonkin. S'ch a man as 'a es for losing of 'n and breaking of 'n. Your baccy's in your purse, father, and your purse in your left trousies pocket, and so's your knife. Mind, when you d' want to spittie g' out to the door, dacent, and liv Mrs Tonkin's clane slab alone. Well, Mrs Tonkin, my dear, and how's fishing?"

124

"Aw – plenty o' fish, 'a b'lieve, plenty."

"Sure?"

"Ess, plenty in the say, trouble is to get 'em out."

The time-honoured pleasantry was well received.

"Ha-ha! Ess to be sure. Hark to Mrs Tonkin father, 'Plenty in the say,' she d' say, 'trouble is t' get 'em out'. Well, that edn' bad – not bad, that edn'. Good 'nough to put in the paper, 'a b'lieve. Father, get your handkercher out o' your coat pocket and blaw your nose to wance, afore there's a haccident. Eh! Mrs Tonkin, I do admire to be'old the way your fingers d' go about that net. In and out, in and out they d' go. That's a big hole theer."

"Them plaguy sharks and dogs!" ejaculated Mrs Tonkin. "Never was a net so full o' holes. But you d' knaw, Miss Penelloe, 'twill be fuller o' holes when 'tes done mending."

"I don't understand your manen, Mrs Tonkin."

"Why, 'tes a sort o' puzzle we fishing people d' 'ave. What is that which the more you mend et, the more et's full o' holes? Answer is, a net – the meshes being holes, in a manner to spake of, you d' see."

"Well now!" cried Miss Penelloe, "that's clever too. Father, d'st hear that? Why, what's the matter wi' ee now father? Do set still and don't fidget."

Mr Penelloe was shifting uneasily on his chair and mournfully shaking his head, while his eyes were fixed on the corner of the room where the clock-case stood.

"Scand'lous!" he exclaimed in a voice of tragic hoarseness. "That theer clock's seventeen minutes slow!"

"Theer!" cried Miss Penelloe delightedly, "that's father all over! One thing 'a d' think upon is clocks and time. Do 'ee mind setten that clock right, Mrs Tonkin? Father won't rest a minute in the same room with a lying clock."

"Dear me!" exclaimed Mrs Tonkin in troubled tones. "I'm vexed, that I am. Gie 'ee my word I thought 'twas c'rrect. I'll get on a cheer and set 'n right to wance."

"Wait a bit," interposed Miss Penelloe. "You don't mind letten father do 'n hisself? 'Twill plaize 'en mighty, and save trouble – father don't need no cheer for the loftiest clock in the kingdom, 'a b'lieve. Go, father, set 'n right, go! Why, 'twas his great height 'at set father to mending clocks. You must know, sir," she continued turning to the lodger, "father's a carpenter by trade. But when 'a was courten mawther up Camborne way, granf'er, who was a clock-maker, said to father one day, 'Jacob,' 'a said, 'tes plain what Providence intended 'ee for, when 'a made 'ee seven foot high – 'twas to mendie eight-day clocks, sure 'nough. Why, look at me. You caan't think the perils I've gone through along o' standen on rotten-legged auld cheers and wee'waw stools, up top o' steers, and all sorts o' risky places. Ay,' says he, 'tes a trade full o' danger for a little chap like me. I d' get my liven on the brink o' destruction, and peril do compass me round about. With your nose in the vitals of a clock,' says grandf'er, 'you don't pay no 'tention to nawthen else. Maybe you see a wheel loose, or somethen, and you get excited and make a step one way or t'other, and there you are on the ground, and lucky ef clock edn' atop of 'ee. But you're made for the business, Jacob,' 'a said to father, 'throwed away, you are, on planen wood and such. Take my

126

advice,' said he, 'make a proper use o' your gifts, and larn to mend clocks'.

"And so father did, though 'a 've always sticked to his carpenter work, being what 'a was brought up to."

"Clocks is my pastime, only my pastime, so to spake," murmured Mr Penelloe, shambling back to his chair.

"Yet there's few d 'knaw more about clocks and their say-cret mysteries 'an father," said his daughter proudly.

"There's a clock wi' a brass face up foreign, nobody caan't manage but he. The people 'at d' b'long to that clock send for father reg'lar, and pay for his travelling and all, every time 'a d' go wrong. Nobody else waan't do for 'em, they must have father. Let's see, father, what's the matter wi' that clock up to Trebollyvean? I knaw 'tes somethen uncom-mon, but I caan't azackly mind what."

"The affliction o' that p'tic'lar clock," said Mr Penelloe slowly, and, as the lodger thought, in rather a pointed tone, "is being like some females, a brae sight too fond of et's own voice."

"Aw, ess, to be sure. Striking, father d'mane," explained his daughter condescendingly.

"Twill start at dead o' night, and work off three days in ten minutes, or 'twill take a fancy to strike seventeen for every hour o' the day."

"Now!" exclaimed Mrs Tonkin, rather over-doing the accent of wonder in her polite anxiety to show that though her hands might be at work on the net, her thoughts were all absorbed in her visitors' story. "Well!" holding up the net, and with knitted brows scanning its surface for rents.

"Sure!" pouncing on a torn spot and attacking it with knife and needle.

"Bless you," Miss Penelloe went on, "clocks d 'ave their ways and fancies, and wakenesses, and obstinatenesses just like Christians. No two clocks alike, 'a b'lieve. But father d' knaw how to manage 'em all. Not but what 'a draw the line somewhere, as we all must. There was a chap come to father once with a guckoo-clock for 'm to mendie, but father said 'No' to wance. 'Bring me a clock 'at do strike proper,' said he, 'and I'll see to 'n, or bring me a clock 'at don't strike at all, and I'll see to 'n, but a clock 'at d' make a noise like the fowls o' the air edn' no clock at all,' says father. 'Caall 'n what you will. I don't hauld wi' no s'ch full-ishness, nor I waan't ha' nawthen to do wi' 'en,' said he."

"Theer, think o' that!" cried Mrs Tonkin, "Wouldn' ha' nawthen to do wi' 'en! Of course 'ee wouldn', Mrs Penelloe, and I do hauld 'ee in honour for 'n. Guckoo clocks, indeed! Such fullishness as we do find in this mortal world!"

"Fullishness you may well say, Mrs Tonkin, and roguish-ness you might say, and wouldn' be fur wrong. The way people be'ave over clocks – well there! – scand'lous, that 'a es! No notion they haven't o' the way to trate 'em. Father d' often say clock sh'd be 'counted the true master in a house. Et says to 'ee, 'Do this, do that,' every time 'a d' strike. 'Seven o'clock, get up, thou sluggard, and lightie the fire. 'Leven o'clock, put the 'taties on. Four o'clock, fill the ket-tle, ef ye plaize. Ten o'clock, go' up to thy chamber, go! But theer!

"Some people think they can chate time by ill-using

clocks. There's Mrs Perry up our way. Laast thing at night she allers put clock on haalf-an-hour, so she may get up betimes in the mornen. Then back et d' go after brukfast, haalf-an-hour slow, to keepie the men from grummlen 'cause dinner's late.

"Then on again, 'cause she do like tay earlier 'an her conscience 'ull let her. And so 'a goes on, making clock tell lies, and then pretending to b'lieve 'en."

"Shameful!" cried Mrs Tonkin, who, by the way, is guilty of similar conduct every day of her life.

Here attention was directed to Mr Penelloe, who was gazing fixedly at the lodger, while he fumbled with his hands on his knees and made abortive efforts to speak.

"Well, what's the matter now father?" asked his daughter. "Spake up, and don't be bashful ef you've anything to say sensible."

Thus encouraged, Mr Penelloe addressed the lodger. "You're somethen of a scholar, sir, I've no doubt. Studied a good deal, 'a b'lieve."

The lodger made a suitably modest reply.

"Then, spaken o' clocks, can you tell me what's your opinion o' Joshua?"

The connection between the subjects was not very apparent to the lodger, and his expression probably showed this. Miss Penelloe came promptly to the rescue.

"Ah, you edn' the first father's puzzled over that, sir. 'Tes a reg'lar c'nundrum wi' he. Joshua the son o' Nun, 'a d' mane, when 'a made the sun stand still in Gibeon."

"What I want to knaw," said Mr Penelloe earnestly, "is

129

this. I've puzzled over et a good bit, Sundays, and other times."

"So 'a has, Mrs Tonkin," interjected Miss Penelloe. "Every time 'a d' take up his Bible, 'a turns to Joshua, chapter ten*, sure 'nough. Book do open nat'ral on the very place every time – 'a 've got so used to 'n, 'a d' seem to knaw."

"And fur's I can understand from what they're a-tellen me, they d' want to make out that these auld ancient Hebrews hadn' no clocks, which don't seem likely, do it?"

The lodger believed, however, that such was the case.

Mr Penelloe meditated. "Seems queer, a world about clocks. How they managed I caan't think. But what I was axen was this. Ef there had been clocks, that theer merracle 'ud ha' set 'em all wrong, wouldn' et?"

The lodger supposed so.

"Unless, maybe, et acted on the clocks too, so to spake, and stopped em?"

The lodger thought this possible.

"Well et beats me, et do," said Mr Penelloe slowly. "Those must ha' been turr'ble unsettlen times to live in. Wouldn' ha' suited me, 'a b'lieve."

So saying, he relapsed into a brown study. But Miss Penelloe was on her feet.

"Come, father, what wi' your chattering, time's getting on, and us must do likewise."

"Not afore you've had a dish o' tay!" cried Mrs Tonkin.

"No, Mrs Tonkin, caan't stop a minute longer."

Mrs Tonkin cannot endure that frivolous intentions of

her guests should interfere with her exercise of the sacred rights of hospitality.

"Set down!" she exclaimed, with commanding – nay, wrathful – emphasis. But Miss Penelloe was obdurate.

"Come, father, come," she said to her parent. "Gie us your pipe. Button up your coat, et's blawen cauld and wisht outside. There!" placing his hat on his head and jamming it firmly down over his eyes. "Good day, Mrs Tonkin, good day, sir. Say good day to the gentleman, father. Ascuse father's simmin' rudeness, sir, in not being quick to say good day. Polite 'a es by nature, but 'a edn' got the art of et so to spake. 'A 've took a great fancy to 'ee really. I can see that from the free way 'a tackled 'ee over Joshua, and 'tedn' everybody father do take a fancy to. Say good day, why don't 'ee, father?"

Mr Penelloe turned his peering gaze on the lodger again.

"But maybe," he said, "the merracle acting all round, as we agreed, when the sun went on, the clocks 'ud ha' started again."

"Theer!" cried Miss Penelloe in ecstasy, "did 'ee ever hear the like? You've hit et father, right 'nough. That's just father's way. 'A edn so quick as some, but 'a d' sit and puzzle, and the wonderful clever notions 'at d' come into his head! But come, go we must."

"Well!" exclaimed Mrs Tonkin when Mr Penelloe had been safely conveyed into the street, and the door had closed on the visitors. "Well! Ded 'ee ever hear s'ch nonsense, wi' their clocks and fullishness? He edn' azackly, I don't think, and as for she, wi' her talk – 'tes enough to put-

131

tie one deef, so a' es. 'A course I was forced to be polite to 'em in my own kitchen, and then you must allow for 'em being from the country, where sense is scarce. But theer!"

Words failed her, and she vented her feeling in a vigorous attack on the net.

"Come! Where's that dish o' tay – come."

It was Mr Tonkin, returning to the attack, and backed up by Jimmy. This time Mrs Tonkin had no objection to raise, and laying down her work, she went to the cupboard.

Looking at the clock, the lodger found that the time, as amended by Mr Penelloe, was half-past three. Foreseeing an invitation to partake, which he must either refuse and grievously offend Mrs Tonkin, or accept to the detriment of his digestion, he thought best to avoid the dilemma by retiring from the scene.

The "lodger" in this story is Lee, while Mrs Tonkin is Elizabeth Simons, his landlady. The house can still be seen at the corner of Fore Street, Newlyn. The description of its interior decoration bears many similarities to that of the Joses' house in *Paul Carah*, which is set in Coverack.

* Joshua Chapter 10 Verse 13: And the sun stood still, and the moon stayed, until the people had avenged themselves upon their enemies. Is not this written in the book of Jasher? So the sun stood still in the midst of heaven, and hasted not to down about a whole day.

THE HEROIC EXPLOITS OF
THE FIVE JOHNS

T HE SEA roared, the wind whistled and five brave
Cornishmen sat round a lantern in a fish cellar
sucking at their pipes. If you had come to the door
and called "John Johns!" five brave Cornishmen would
have started to their feet; but among themselves, to avoid
all possible confusion, they were John, Johnny, Jack, Jacky
and Jan.

John was Johnny's father, Jacky was Jack's son and Jan
claimed a more or less complicated relationship with all
four.

The word was with Jack.

"Ess," he said, "three kegs of brandy picked up a mile
west of Penzour, and two kegs of brandy and a puncheon
of rum washed in 'pon the rocks over to Penriskey beach.
And the coastguardsmen, dear souls, got the lot."

"The good things of this life is wasted on the onde-
servin'," said John, and spat with mournful reflectiveness.

"What's a puncheon?" asked Johnny, whose youth
excused his ignorance.

"Puncheon's the biggest kind o' barr'l that is a barr'l,"
explained his father. "Idn' that so, Jack?"

"That's of it. And the rum in this one was so white as

milk, so they tell me; and that strong, one of the coastguard got drunk with smelling to the bunghole."

"A cheap drunk, that," said Jan.

"Cheap, sure 'nough," agreed Jack. "But onsatisfactory."

"Look!" said Jacky, suddenly. Alone of the five he was in sea going fig-high boots and dripping oil-skins. "Look! When I was hauling pots this evenin', over by Guckoo Rock, I thought I see something floating. Couldn' make it out for the time, but now I come to think 'twas terrible like a g'eat barr'l."

Four pairs of feet shuffled under the stress of deep emotion.

"Over by Guckoo Rock?" ruminated John. "How's the tide?"

"Tide's just making," said Jacky.

John reflected further, and spoke with weighty emphasis.

"That barr'l," he said, "if 'tis a barr'l, will be coming in 'pon Cannel beach, three o'clock tomorrow morning."

"That's so," said Jack. "And the look-out man up to Beriskey'll be along that way from four to half-past, and if 'tis there, he'll have en."

"And if 'tidn', he won't," said John.

"Who'll jine me for a stroll along cliff bimeby?" asked Jack.

"My legs," said John, "is feeling a bit stiff. A bit of a walk'll make 'em pliant. So I'll come for one, and Johnny for another."

"'Tis a dark night," said Jacky. "Mother'd be brave and anxious if I left father go walking alone. So I'll come too."

"The missus," said Jan, "have got a bad cowld on her chest. And when she've got a cowld on her chest she snore like thunder. Might so well go for a walk as lay a-bed listening to she."

"Rogues do walk by night," said John. "If we should hap to meet one, I'll bring an axe to smash en with."

"A rope 'ud be handy to tie en up with arterwards," said Jan. "I'll bring the rope."

Jack pulled out his watch.

"Nine o'clock," he said, rising. "Tidn' down in the 'rithmetic books that nine and six is three, but you'll understand my maning. Good-night all."

"Good-night."

And five brave Cornishmen rolled their ways homeward.

Six hours later, five brave Cornishmen picked their cautious steps down a steep cliff-path and stumbled among rocks and pebbles to the verge of a little sandy beach. All was black around them; before them a dim grey line wavered and shifted, and out of the line came a voice of thunder incessantly shouting. The five advanced with a thin salt rain beating against their faces, and stood in an equal-spaced row, peering seawards.

Long they stood, nor saw what they hoped to see, till the grey line whitened and vague shapes of clouds appeared driving overhead, black against a lesser blackness. Jack displayed annoyance.

"Day's breaking abroad," he said. "Plaguy old barr'l! Where's it to?"

Suddenly Johnny shouted. His shoulder was against his

cheek, and his arm and hand and forefinger were one rigid
bar, pointing seawards.

"There 'tis! That's of it!" he cried.

The row became a huddled group.

"Stand by!" bawled Jan, advancing knee-deep into the
surf, and slipping the coils of the rope from his shoulder to
his left hand, while with his right he grasped the grapnel
that was attached to the end.

Twice he cast and missed; the third time he yelled and
jerked a fathom of rope-end behind him. Eight ready hands
clutched it.

"Heave – in with her!" chorused the five Johns, and a
mighty bulk came rolling in among them. They hauled it
out of the surf, and stood around it, gloating and taking
breath.

"My life, what a tremenjous g'eat barr'l!" exclaimed
Johnny.

"A puncheon, sure 'nough," said Jacky.

"Never see such a tremenjous barr'l," said Jan. "How's
going to haul en over cliff?"

"Tidn' to be done – not in the dark by we," said John
mournfully.

"Where's going to hide en, then?" asked Jan.

"Tidn' to be done – not on this li'll dinky beach," said
John, still more mournfully.

"Tis just the way of Providence," reflected Johnny.
"Nothing, or else too much. What's to be done?"

"Who'll fetch the coastguard?" said Jacky with a bitter
laugh.

"Foolishness!" exclaimed Jack. "You do talk sick. Come, my dears, haul her up under the cliff, and then we'll see."

They rolled the barrel off the sand and in among the rocks.

"Now," said Jack. "This barr'l belong to Gov'ment. We'm law-abiding Cornishmen, and don't cheat nobody o' their lawful doo – not even Gov'ment. Gov'ment shall have his barr'l whenever he choose to fetch en. But, seeming to me" – he took out a clasp-knife – "seeming to me, barr'l's onfort'nitly sprung a leak – or going to; and nobody's fault, nuther, considering what he've gone through lately."

He began to carve at the bung.

"I haven' been drunk, not since Band of Hope meeting last Christmas," said John, moistening his lips. "I always get drunk then," he explained, "to show I an't one of 'em."

"I'm a teetotaller as a rule," said Jan. "But I trust to be able to do my duty by a wreck so well as any little-drop man among 'e."

Blop! A delicious fragrance diffused itself around.

"Rum, or I'm a Dutchman!" cried Jack, and produced a tin pannikin from under his guernsey. Jacky tilted the barrel, and the generous liquor flowed. Jack tasted.

"Genuine Jamaica!" he exclaimed, and drained the pannikin, and refilled it, and drained it again.

"Turn about!" expostulated John.

"No, 'a b'lieve," said Jack, "This here's a hoff-licence. Jugs and bottles only."

"Here!" exclaimed John. "This won't do. Us can't drink out o' the bunghole. Hand over the pannikin, will 'e?"

The pannikin was at Jack's lips. He shook his head, and a wink was obscurely visible in the grey dawn. John forced a laugh.

"A joke's a joke," he said. "The barr'l may be Gov'ment's, but the liquor's ourn – ourn so much as yourn. Hand over that pannikin."

"My pannikin," said Jack simply.

John grew hot and threatening.

"Us didn' turn out of our beds in no weather 'tall, just to see a greedy old rogue get drunk. Once for all, hand over that pannikin, or –."

A shout from Jan saved the situation. He had been searching among the rubbish at high water mark, and now he hurried back triumphant with two empty condensed milk tins, the bottom of a broken beer bottle, and a scallop shell.

"Never again will I say a word agin Providence!" said Johnny fervently.

The vessels were distributed, and for a while no sound was heard but the gurgle of liquor flowing out and in. Jacky found the office of tilting the barrel a thankless one, and a hindrance to business.

So its position was altered and the liquor was allowed to flow in a continuous stream. There was always a receptacle ready to catch it, and little was wasted.

Soon it was found inconvenient to stand upright, and the five devotees were constrained to kneel or sit about the fountain.

Suddenly Jan swerved as he knelt; the milk-tin slipped

from his grasp, and with a high-pitched maidenly giggle he fell prostrate.

"There now!" said Jack, his voice thick with disgust. "See what comes o' this t-tee-teetotalish nonsenshe!"

Johnny was mumbling to himself, his brow wrinkled with anger. The incessant uproar of the waves was giving him deep offence.

"Plaguy old say!" he muttered. "Make en sing 'nother tune, so I will!"

Stumbling to his feet, he made three steps with a threatening arm upraised, and fell safely into a bed of seaweed.

THE STRANGER AND THE ARCHDEACON

IT WAS a bell ringers' festival in a small Cornish village. The occasion was the inauguration of a new peal of bells in the church tower. The programme consisted of first a ringing competition between five celebrated teams of campanologists, secondly a ninepenny tea in the school-room, and in the evening a dedication service, at which an Archdeacon was to officiate. What I have to tell of occurred at the tea.

The schoolroom was furnished with four long tables. At each end of each table, with urn, kettle, and cups before her, stood one who seemed a daughter of the Gods – such haughty transformation does the public dispensing of liquid nourishment, be it tea or beer, mysteriously work in womankind.

Along the tables, crowded as close as mortals could be crowded, and breathe, sat a heterogeneous company of farm and fisher folk – members of three or four villages and a dozen scattered town places – all devoutly engaged in justifying the ninepence. The farther end of the farthest table was reserved for the Rector's party of quality folk, to whom that ninepence was plainly as nothing, for they talked more than they ate, deliberately chose the thinnest slices of bread and butter, and eschewed the cake altogether. There I spied a gap in the ranks, and took my seat therein.

I found myself face to face with the Archdeacon himself. The Rector's wife was on one side of him, and on the other sat a lentorn-jawed stranger, who was eating and drinking with the desperate determination of the incurably thin man. It was impossible not to admire the easy nonchalance with which he reached across the Archdeacon, and dipped his spoon, half full of tea, into the sugar-basin, right under the formidable nose of the Rector's wife.

Admirable, too, was his prescient promptitude in taking toll of their rarer dainties – saffron cakes, jam tarts, and the like – as they travelled to and fro before him, and storing them for future consumption on the subsidiary plate which he guarded within the crook of his elbow.

Presently, having drained his cup, he marked it for his own by taking two jammy plum stones from his plate, sucking them dry, and depositing them in the saucer. Then half-rising, he balanced himself with one hand on the Archdeacon's shoulder, and with the other steered cup and saucer along the table between plates and dishes, as far in the direction of the tea-urn as his extended finger could reach. There he abandoned them trustingly to the care and guidance of the gentry, and sinking back in his seat, looked about him for the first time.

There was a fit opportunity to devote a few moments to the lighter amenities of the social board, and he began by addressing a general observation to the company at large, as one who casts a line at random in unknown waters.

"Friends," he said, "let us be truly thankful there's one tasty tipple on the land that don't make a man drunk."

The Archdeacon beamed mildly round upon him. Thus encouraged, he plunged at once into a confidential intimacy with his venerable neighbour.

"Though there's some in these parts, mister," he remarked, laying a familiar forefinger on the other's arm, "that take gin to their tay, and I shouldn't wonder but that you know plenty that do the same."

"A bad habit," said the Archdeacon, without committing himself to an acknowledgement of disreputable acquaintance.

"So 'tis. A wasteful habit. It spoil the tay, and don't improve the gin. To my mind, gin be poor trade at the best o' times. Cheap, says you, and I grant 'e that. If you've a mind to be drunk, 'twill serve your turn, but when I come across a man that don't consider the quality of this liquor, don't matter who he is, I condemn that man for a perishing beast.

"The drink's the thing, not the drunk, bear that in mind. Ess, a wasteful habit, and what's more, a mean, deceitful habit. Get drunk if you've a mind to, says I, but do it honest and open like."

The stranger's voice was loud and clear. By this time half the room was listening absorbedly. His attitude, his intent eye and impressive forefinger, gave his remarks such a disconcerting air of personal remonstrance, that the Archdeacon was hardly to be blamed for abruptly changing the subject.

143

"This is an interesting occasion on which we are met together today," said he.

"So 'tis," agreed the stranger. "Though I set more store by supper myself."

"I was referring to the bell-ringing," explained the Archdeacon in haste.

"Oh, that! Ay! Well, to tell 'e the truth, I didn' come in time for that, nor I didn' look to, nuther. I pitched to get here in time for the tay. Mind'e, I'm Primitive myself, but whenever there's a Church tay and wine on – well, call me a carnal-minded backslider if you like, but I'm there.

"Our Primitive tays ben't much account, you see. We haven' got the cash, and that's the truth. We may be rich in doctrine, few more so, but our pastry's poor stuff. Wesleyan tays an't no better.

"They're a mean lot, these Wesleyans. If ever you go to a Wesleyan tay, mister, whatever you do, don' go to double your slice, or not a taste o' the butter you'll get 'pon your tongue, they scrape it that thin. Now Baptists is a bit better. I've knowed some tidy Baptist come-outs. There's gen'rally tarts. Ess, and crame at a particular time. But when it come to the flesh-pots, give me church."

His speculative eye wandered over the Archdeacon's comely propositions, and that embarrassed ecclesiastic toyed nervously with the crumbs on his plate. The stranger's glance was directed to the plate.

"But you an't ateing nothing!" he exclaimed with genuine concern. "A wisht poor ninepenn'orth you're putting away, b'lieve. "Ninepenn'orth," says I, "but I reckon they passed 'e in free, seeing as how you'm giving 'em a discoorse this avening, so I'm towld."

The Archdeacon shook his head. "They made me pay my ninepence," he said with a feeble smile.

"More shame to they, then, when 'tis written that the labourer's worthy of his hire. If you can't pitch 'em ninepen'orth o' doctrine, you must be a poor praicher, sure 'nough. Well, you might as well get your value for your money, while you'rn about it. Here," – he seized a plate at random – "try these here saffern cakes. I never put my teeth into solider cakes, not in my life, I assure 'e."

"Too heavy for me, I fear," said the Archdeacon, politely waving away the proffered dish.

"Wake stummick?" queried the other sympathetically. "Indigestion, I shouldn' wonder. Well, 'tis a sore burden. There's a man in our locality that's plagued terrible that way, and he's in your line o' business too. He's local praicher up to Bible Christian chapel, William Robbins is, and love hot potato cake better 'n hot potato cake love he. Sure as he should put a mossel 'pon his tongue, the stummick do rise and rage.

"But William don't pay no 'tention, he'd scorn to be a slave to his organs, William would. So sure's Sunday do come round, there's a hot potato cake smoking 'pon William's table, and there's William pitching and haiving 'way to en like a thrashing-machine. 'Mortifying the flesh', he do call it, being a spiritual man, as I said. And when he've got to deliver a discoorse, then 'tis double 'lowance with he, and the worse the indigestion do take en, the bet-

145

ter 'a do praich. 'Suffering's good for the soul', says William, shovelling away. 'There's nothing,' says he, 'do set a man groaning under conviction quicker 'n a grievous pain inside,' says he. 'Spaking in parables, tis the cup o' water that do start the pump,' says William, and I shouldn' wonder but that he's right.

"You take my advice, mister, and take a good stiff tay, your discoorse won't suffer by em, I promise 'e. Mortify the flesh, mister, 'coording to what William do say, and you'll find, when you climb up in the pulpit, your speret'll soar like a say-gull."

A cup was passed to the distracted Archdeacon. Absently he took it, and mechanically he began to stir its contents. The manner of the stranger changed.

"Excuse me, mister," he said, politely stern. "I allow 'tis tejous having to wait the time they keep 'e here. But that an't no excuse for trying to come in out o' your turn. If you'll look inside that saucer, you'll find two plummy-stones. I put 'em there myself. That there cup o' tay's my cup o' tay, and I'll trouble 'e hand en over, if you'll be so kind."

So saying, and paying no heed to the Archdeacon's babbled apologies, he seized the cup in one hand and a slice of cake in the other, and relapsed into busy silence. The spell was lifted from the room, cups cleared again, and plates of eatables revolved once more in their orbits. The Archdeacon drew a breath, brushed his forehead, turned to the Rector's wife, and chirruped a brisk inquiry about the Mothers' Meetings.

I whispered the natural question to my neighbour, a fisherman with whom I had some acquaintance. The answer came harshly from behind a huge hand.

"Bendigo Drew, shoemaker up to Polgoose. Larned the owld chap a thing or two, didn' 'a? Aw! – he's a masterpiece, Bendigo is. He's the man that Simons up to St Kenna sent round the notice for, by town-crier. Heard tell o' that? No? Well, Simons do keep a' ateing-house, with a shilling ordinary 'pon market days. Notice was to this effeck and so forth: Simons' celebrated shilling ordinary, come one, come all, and Bendigo Drew likeways, if he've a mind to. But Bendigo've got to pay by the plateful. Aw – a masterpiece! For ateing, drinking and discoorse a complete masterpiece is Bendigo."

THE THREE OLD GENTLEMEN

TO THIS day, Mrs Jane, brooding over the strange
incident that disturbed the even monotony of her
life, oscillates between two opinions – either the
three old gentlemen were stark mad, or else for twenty
years she had played a fool's game, blindly throwing a gold-
en treasure piece by piece into the gutter, under the impression that it was common brass.

The former theory is the more plausible and comfortable, and it is the only one she has ever broached in public.
But there are times when a horrid doubt possesses her soul,
and every detail of the fantastic occurrence points a jeering
finger at her self-respect. Luckily for her, that doubt can
never become a certainty. A curtain of dubious mystery
hangs perplexingly over the story, and the magic worked
which might remove it was not uttered in her presence, a
door between. True the door had a keyhole, but what warning had she?

Mrs Jane is, and has been for thirty years, mistress of the
White Bull, an ancient inn in the churchtown of
Perranveor. The White Bull is the only hostelry Perranveor
can boast of, for though, possessing a church, it is dignified
with the title of "town" in Cornish parlance, it is in fact
only a small village of small cottages, set, Cornish fashion,
on a hilltop, in a lonely district of upland pastures. No

place, even in that land of solitary communities, is so remote from the world as Perranveor.

It is ten miles from the railway, twelve from the nearest market town. There is nothing in the neighbourhood to attract the visitors who swarm over Cornwall in increasing numbers every year. The Druids, who have done so much for other parts of the country, have basely neglected Perranveor. Not a circle, not a solitary cromlech, to help it to a line in the guide books. Even King Arthur had unaccountably passed it over, and Tregeagle, that ubiquitous villain, knew it not.

Once it had a mine, but that has long since gone the way of Cornish mines. It has no resident gentry, the squire lives "foreign" and the parson – who is rector of both Perranveor and Perranoze – resides at the latter place, and leaves Perranveor to its own devices, except for two hours on alternate Sunday evenings. No one comes to Perranveor, and no one leaves it, except in the course of nature.

The one noteworthy event of Mrs Jane's life, before the coming of the three old gentlemen, had been her marriage to Ben Jane – not that Ben, or the fact of his marrying her, was to be accounted an event. Marriage is only an incident, and Ben was of no account at all. But it transplanted her from one end of the village to the other, and it was years before the uneasy feeling of sojourning in foreign parts wore off.

When the extraordinary event of which you are to hear took place, she had been twenty years mistress of the White Bull, and of those twenty years not one was to be distinguished from another. Every Saturday night Angove the smith got drunk on sampson, which is a mixture of cider and brandy, and Mitchell the shopkeeper got drunk on mahogany, which is a mixture of gin and treacle. And every Saturday night they quarrelled in their cups.

Every day the same faces showed over the little bar, called for the same liquors, talked the same talk, and cracked the same jokes. A peaceful, uneventful existence was Ellen Jane's at the White Bull.

The coming of the three old gentlemen, and their incredible behaviour in the inn-parlour, stands out in her memory against the dull stretch of years before and after, much as the vivid red of their coats stood out against the neutral tints of the February twilight, when they came riding into Perranveor.

For it was towards dusk on a February evening, as she stood idle at the door of the inn, that she saw them approaching, walking their tired horses up the steep village street. Nobody was about. The men were not home from work yet, nor the children from school, and the women were within-doors, boiling the kettles for tea. Up the street they came, looking curiously about them. When they came to the crossroads by the blacksmith's shanty, they halted and conferred, peering this way and that.

Then one of them caught sight of Mrs Jane, distinct in her white apron against the dark doorway, and all three came riding towards her, the big fat old gentleman, the long thin old gentleman and the little old gentleman. So, in her narrative, she distinguished them, being ignorant to this day of their names. Before the door they stopped, and the fat one addressed her, asking the name of the village. She told him and he turned a look of enquiry on the others, who shook their heads.

"And how far is it to Truro?" he asked.

"Thirteen mile, 'a b'lieve, sir," said Mrs Jane.

The fat one swore heartily.

"What's to be done?" he said to his companions. "The horses can't do it without a rest."

"I should be glad of a rest myself," said the thin one. "That last run was awful, never knew anything like it. Not sure if I could manage thirteen more miles!"

The three looked dubiously at the squalid ale-house front.

Mrs Jane plucked up courage.

"If you'll please to step inside for a bit," she said nervously. "Edn' a place for quality, I d'know, but if I'm mean, I'm clean."

"But the horses?" said the thin one. "Is there a man about?"

"Aw ess," said Mrs Jane, "there's a man. Edn' much of a man, but 'e's a man f'rall that."

The three conferred.

"Very well," said the fat one. "Produce your man."

Mrs Jane disappeared for a moment and returned with her husband. The three old gentleman dismounted, delivered their horses over to his care, and followed Mrs Jane into the inn parlour.

A long desk table, some benches of like material, a sand-ed floor, some nightmare points and almanacs, and a close odour of stale beer and tobacco – thus such was the parlour of the White Bull.

The three old gentleman sat heavily down in a row on one of the benches, and looked at Mrs Jane as she stood before them. There was a fire in the grate, which lit up their red hunting coats, and their ruddy faces, making a great show of colour in the dusky room. And there they sat and looked at her. She felt very nervous. Quality on horseback was disconcerting enough, quality dismounted, and sitting in expectant poses on her premises, and staring at her was paralysing. She wished she had not invited them in.

"Maybe the gentlemen 'ud like something' to drink," she suggested timidly.

"Of course we would, my good woman," said the fat one heartily.

"If you have anything fit to drink," added the thin one.

Mrs Jane bridled.

"I'd have 'ee know, sir, I brew my own ale myself," she said, as bold as you please, "an' there edn' better ale nowheres."

"Bring some ale then," said the fat one.

The little one nodded as Mrs Jane sought his eye, but the thin one shook his head.

"No disparagement intended to your brewing, ma'am," he said, "but I'm not of an adventurous temper. What else?"

"There's cider –" began Mrs Jane.

"Also your own brewing? No, I won't have cider."

Mrs Jane was at her wit's end. She couldn't suggest sampson or mahogany to such particular old gentlemen.

"What would 'ee fancy, sir?" she said despairingly.

"Well, ma'am," said he, "since you are so polite as to enquire, I should like a pint of claret." Then he chuckled, and the fat one chuckled and the little one chuckled.

Mrs Jane saw a ray of hope.

"Don' know 'bout claret," she said, "but there's some wine in the house. I wouldn' ha' spoken of et, on'y there edn' nothen' else I can offer 'ee."

"Wine?" said the three old gentlemen in a breath.

"Pooh!" said the thin one. "Elder or currant."

"No," said Mrs Jane, "a edn' elder nor 'a edn' currant, nor I don't know what 'a es. Been here a brae while – longer 'n I've been. But 'a edn' no account at all. I couldn' get rids of en ef I didn' sell en cheap. Yaller stuff, 'a es, an' sixpence gallon's all the men'll pay fur'n. Cider's eightpence, so that'll tell 'ee. Wash, they d' call en, not havin' no name fur'n."

The three old gentlemen seemed curiously interested. They looked at each other, and exchanged some remarks in a low tone. Mrs Jane caught a few words. The fat one said something about "a find" while the thin one exclaimed quite distinctly "Pooh! Mare's-nest!" Then the fat one turned to her and said: "Never mind about the ale for the present, bring us a jug of 'wash' and some glasses."

Mrs Jane protested. It wasn't fit stuff for quality to drink. The men of the town wouldn't look at it till they were too drunk to care what they were swallowing. But the old gentlemen peremptorily insisted, and she departed to carry out their orders.

Returning with jug and glasses, she set the tray down on the table and hurried out and shut the door, fearing the inevitable explosion of wrath and disgust at the first sip of the mucky stuff.

One minute passed, and two, and three, and still no sound came from the little parlour. Then a violent peel of the bell brought her heart into her mouth. She knew what it meant. It was for ale to wash the taste out. Farmer Bodilly had acted in precisely the same way when they persuaded him to try the stuff. Quickly she drew a jug of her home-brewed, put it on the tray with clean glasses, and hastened into the parlour.

The three old gentlemen were standing at the table. The little one held in his hand a glass half full of the "wash", to which he was alternately sniffing and sipping. The other two watched him intently. The fat one was quite purple in the face, the thin one very pale. Mrs Jane noticed, too, that the glass which the little one held shook as if his hand was trembling. For a moment no one noticed her, then the little one put the glass down tenderly, and returned a solemn nod to the inquiring looks of the other two.

"Extraordinary!" said the fat one. "Incredible!" said the thin one. Then they turned to Mrs Jane.

"Now madam," said the fat old gentleman, "I'll trouble you –" Here he saw what she was carrying, and broke off. "What's that for?" he cried.

Mrs Jane explained that she thought he had rung for ale.

"And why the deuce should you think that?" he thundered.

Mrs Jane offered further explanations, quoting Farmer Bodilly as a precedent. To her utter amazement, the three old gentlemen burst into a roar of laughter. It was then that a doubt of their sanity first entered her mind.

Recovering himself, the fat one had her set the tray down and shut the door.

"And now, ma'am," he said, "I want you to answer a few questions. You say that this" – pointing to the 'wash' – "has been here a long time. Have you any notion where it came from, and how it came here?"

"Well," said Mrs Jane cautiously, "I don't know for certain, but I could gie a brae guess, maybe."

"Come," said the fat one, "sit down and tell us all you know about it. It will be worth your while."

Thus encouraged, Mrs Jane launched out into history.

"Thirty year ago," she said, "there was a g'eat storm in these parts, an' the wind unfiffled the thatch o' this 'ouse – snatched en clean off. That was in auld Isaac Jane's days – my 'usband's father. So nex' day, when the wind had gone down, auld Isaac he took a ladder an' climbed up to see how much damage was done. An' 'a found a sort o' holler place in the roof, over by the chimney, an' in that holler place he be'old two g'eat barr'ls full o' this here wine. An' they do say they were put there in the auld smugglers' days – brought up by the smugglers from Lanhole River, an' hided there.

"An' some do think that the men that did it must have

got catched an' sent to Bodmin soon arter, an' nobody else knowed about the barr'ls an' there they'd been ever since, clane forgot. But auld Isaac he fetched the barr'ls down an' put 'em in the cellar, an' there they are now. Maybe 'et was good stuff in them barr'ls wance – must ha' been, or they wouldn' ha' hided 'em so careful. But, 'couse, been keeped all that while – 'most a hundred year, they d' say – all the stren'th an' goodness is clane gone out of en."

The three old gentlemen listened with a most gratifying show of attention – with an interest, indeed, that seemed out of all proportion to the claims of the story. It was flattering, but puzzling. Even now, as she rose to leave them, the fat one stopped her.

"Wait a bit," he said. "Two barrels, you said? How much do they hold?"

"About fifty gallons aich, sir," said she.

"A hundred gallons!" he ejaculated. And the thin one and the little one echoed him.

"A hundred gallon!"

She began to be alarmed at their strange excitement. Their eyes glistened, their tongues moved to and fro on their lips, their cheeks were unnaturally flushed. She strove to calm them by removing the apparent cause.

"There wor a hundred gallon," she said, "but the men have drunk a brae lot, these twenty year. Edn' much more'n eight gallon left, or may be ten."

"Good God!" gasped the fat one, and the thin one swore roundly, while the little one sat suddenly down as if he was taken bad.

157

"Good God!" the fat one repeated. "Wasted on these clowns and clodhoppers! Poured into the gutter!" He turned fiercely on Mrs Jane. "You wretched woman!" he began, "do you know what you've done?"

But the little one laid a hand on his arm.

"She doesn't know," he said, "and she needn't know. Don't be alarmed, ma'am," he continued to Mrs Jane, who stood petrified. "You are not to blame, far from it. On the contrary, I would venture to assert that no landlady since the world began ever treated her customers so generously. You shall not go unrewarded." He stood up and bowed. "I will purchase what remains of this wine – we will call it ten gallons, and I will pay you your own price for it."

At the introduction of business, Mrs Jane recovered her wits temporarily. She made a rapid calculation.

"Ten gallon," she said, "at sixpence, a'll be five shillen, sir, if that edn' too much."

The little one fumbled in his pocket.

"Stop!" roared the fat one. "I'll give you ten shillings."

"A pound!" shouted the thin one.

"Two pounds!" yelled the fat one.

"Five!" squeaked the little one.

"Ten!"

"Twenty!"

"Thirty!"

"Fifty pounds!"

They were glaring ferociously at each other. Terror succeeded amazement in Mrs Jane's countenance. She forgot her manners.

"My life!" she exclaimed faintly. "Are 'ee all gone mazed together?"

"Come," said the little one, controlling himself. "This won't do. If you'll kindly leave us for a moment, madam, we will discuss this little matter between ourselves."

Pale and dumb, Mrs Jane tottered from the room and sank on a chair in the bar. What was she to do, alone and unprotected – Ben didn't count – with these three red-coated lunatics in the house?

The bell rang, and in fear and trembling she presented herself. The fat one was again the spokesman.

"We have decided, ma'am," he said, "to make you a joint offer. We are willing to purchase what you have left of the wine, and we will give you the fifty pounds you have already been offered. Does that satisfy you?"

Mrs Jane gasped.

"Well, ma'am?" said the fat one impatiently.

"Edn' jokin' are 'ee?" she murmured feebly.

"Madam, I assure you we are not. Yes or no?"

"Ess, then!" she cried desperately, "an' the Lord forgie me for taking' advantage o' your fullishness!"

"Don't let that distress you for a moment," said he. "Now, take the tray with the wine, and show us down into the cellar."

"Aw, my nerves, what next?" was Mrs Jane's mental comment, but the thought of her unprotected slate, and of the fifty pounds, kept her lips sealed. Without a word she led them out of the room and down a narrow flight of steps into the cellar.

"Where is it?" said the fat one, and she pointed silently to a barrel. He took a glass from the tray, approached the barrel, drew off a thimbleful of the golden liquor, and tested it with nose and tongue. He handed the glass to the others and they did likewise, with subdued and reverent demeanour. Then, uncorking the bung hole, he carefully poured every drop that remained in the jug and the two glasses back into the barrel, and demanded wax. In a walking dream Mrs Jane brought wax. He tore his handkerchief into strips and fastened the strips down over tap and bung hole with the wax, and sealed the wax with the signet ring he wore on the little finger of his left hand.

"Tomorrow," he said, "my brother will call with the money. You will show him down here, and give him any assistance he may require in removing the wine. And now, ma'am, will you have our horses brought to the door?"

They mounted and rode off. Mrs Jane watched, straining her eyes, until the three red patches melted into the gloom, and then her overstrained nerves gave way, and for the first and last time in her life she went off into a violent fit of hysterics. It is left to your imagination to picture the wild excitements that pervaded Perranveor that night – the frantic conjectures, the heated discussions, the minute and repeated examinations Mrs Jane underwent, in the hope of recovering some slight unregarded word, dropped by one of the three, which might give a clue to the mystery.

The White Bull was crowded as it had never been crowded before. Joe Harvey, the village drunkard, who had been converted from his evil ways at the Revival only a month

ago, slid back from the path of righteousness and absti-
nence without an effort to save himself.

A continuous procession of men and women was march-
ing down into the cellar all the evening, there to inspect
with their own eyes the wonderful barrel with its bonds and
seals. Men were seen standing apart, thoughtfully rolling
their tongues about their mouths, striving, it is supposed,
to recall the taste of the magic liquor. And one and all
resolved to be on the scene next day when the fat old gentlemen's brother arrived.

It was midday when a smart trap drove up to the White
Bull in the presence of the assembled population. Now Mrs
Jane had declared the night before, when the stir of conjec-
ture was at its height, that they might leave it to her.
Quality were one thing, quality's servants were another. Let
them wait until the butler came – she would fooch it all out
of him, never fear. She would tackle him. A glass, an artful
question or two, and the thing was done.

But when the trap stopped at her door, and there
descended from the box a grand gentleman in black, with
a gold watch chain and an awe-inspiring demurrer, she
realised at once how futile was her plan. Impossible to
cross-question in the familiar way she had proposed, this dignified personage, whose speech was as precise and lordly as his
attire, who, in his whole appearance and behaviour, corre-
sponded far more closely with her preconceived notions of the
nobility than did his hearty, red-faced, bull-voiced master.

In awed silence she conducted him to the cellar. In awed
silence she watched him take off his coat, turn up his

immaculate cuffs, and set to work, with a priest-like solemnity, to draw off the liquor into the two big flagons he had brought with him. In awed silence she received the ten crackling bank notes from his plump white hands, and curtsied low as she took them.

No other was the effect he produced on the assembled multitude, when he issued from the inn door, followed by Mrs Jane and her husband, each bearing a flagon. Voices were hushed and shifting feet were still, as the little procession moved across the yard with a slow ceremonial gravity. The flagons were deposited in the trap, the grand gentleman mounted on the box seat and took the reins.

Then, at the last moment, Mitchell the shopkeeper shook himself free of the spell, and, pushing through the crowd, seized the horse's head.

"Look, maister!" he shouted, "us do wan' to know the manner of all this here come-out. What's the name o' this here stuff? What do 'ee want wed'n? Aw!"

"Stand aside, my man," said the grand gentleman, and flicked the horse with his whip. The horse sprang forward, Mitchell skipped aside and in a moment horse, trap, grand gentleman and wine vanished forever from the ken of Perranveor, and all hope of solving the mystery was at an end.

But somewhere in Cornwall dwell three squires, who sometimes tell their guests after dinner a strange tale of an aged wine beyond price, rescued by a miraculous chance from an ignoble destiny. And if the company be select and few, the butler may be beckoned to, and bidden to fetch a bottle of that old Madeira.

TELEGRAMS – THE NEW VANG

N OWADAYS, I hear, Port Oliver boasts of a big
hotel furnished from the Tottenham Court Road;
and even with that, and a terrace of new lodging
houses, it is hard put to accommodate the crowd of summer visitors.

But when I was there some ten or a dozen years ago, it
was still the remotest and most primitive of Cornish fishing villages. I had some difficulty in finding it at all.
Tramping the nine miles from the nearest railway station, I
got entangled in an intricate labyrinth of lanes, from which
I was extricated at last, like Theseus, by a thread.

"Follow the telegraph," said the decrepit, black-goggled
road-mender, pointing to the single wire that ran down the
narrowest of the five turnings, in the midst of which he sat
on his heap of stones, like a spider in her web.

I followed it, and came at last to my destination.

Thirty or forty cottages, white-walled and brown-
thatched, huddled one above another in a cliff-cranny,
great bushes of fuchsia and lauslistinus abloom behind
green palings, a clean smell of seaweed, a serried array of
boats poking their sterns up a steep narrow street, a little
weather-beaten quay circling an arm about a streak of yellow sand and green water, on the quay a group of sea-gods,
dark-haired, immobile, and beyond all an infinite blue sea,

flecked with white – such were my first impressions of Port Oliver.

Inquiries put me on the track of Mrs Dawe, who "did sometimes take a gentlemen". Mrs Dawe was reluctant at first; her rooms were not in a fit state to accommodate gentlefolk; the parlour chimney smoked, the bedroom hadn't been spring-cleaned, and the whole house was "like a bird cage for draughts". But I was used to the coy ways of the Cornish landlady, and with a firm front and a pathetic appeal to her mercy on behalf of a homeless wanderer, I continued at last to vanquish her scruples.

Next morning there were letters to despatch, and stamps were needed. I found the post office in a small cottage differentiated from its neighbours only by the usual Government sign-board, and knocking at the closed door, I was bidden to step inside.

The door opened straight into the kitchen, and it was somewhat embarrassing to find that I had intruded on a domestic scene of a most intimate nature. An old man sat at the table, munching his midday pasty, and down by the fire knelt a young woman, washing a baby in a tin bath. I stammered an apologetic allusion to postage stamps.

The postmaster – for such he was – nodded, wiped his mouth on his fingers and his fingers on his knees, and went across to the door of the little parlour. The young woman, after giving me a smile and word of greeting, went on unconcernedly with her maternal duties.

The postmaster returned with the stamps. He eyed me narrowly as he handed them over.

"You'm the young chap that's staying up to Sarah Dawe's," he said.

There was no denying this.

"Come straight from London, so I hear."

This too I had to admit.

"'Tis a long journey. Your mother, now – left your mother home?"

I had.

"She'll be brave and anxious to know you've arrived safe. That a letter for her you've got in your hand?"

It was.

"Post's gone this half-hour. Won't get en till day arter tomorrow, and she fretting her heart out all the while, I'll be bound. You know how 'tis with these women – always fancying things. Now look'n I'll tell 'e what you should do. Send her a tallygram. Won't cost 'e much, and 'twill hearten her up fine. We got a handsome new machine in there, and my married daughter here know how to manage en proper."

I thanked him, but really didn't think –

"Aw, come now! Consider your poor fond mother, as a young man should. What's sixpence, or even a shilling, put it agin a mother's peace o'mind? I'll get 'e a paper."

Off he went, and returned with a telegraph form and a stub of pencil.

"There," he said, thrusting them into my hands.

"Write en off to once, you. No trouble 'tall; I'll tell 'e what to say. 'Arrived safe all well pleasant journey best love' that's about the style of it, 'a b'lieve; short and sweet,

165

like Aunt Mana's pie-crust. Only mind'n – stops is extry."

There was no resisting this. I went to the table and wrote, he leaning over my shoulder.

"That's of it? A prettier hand for a tallygram I never see. No trouble to polish that off. Now, Bessie, show the young chap what you can do."

Bessie arose from her knees, pulled down her sleeves and went into the other room, leaving the half-clad baby kicking and crowing on the floor. The postmaster caught my arm and whispered hoarsely in my ear: "Tis agin the rules, but if you like I'll leave the door abroad, so you can see her working of it off. There, stand just so. Sh! Now she's calling of 'em up. Answer back; all clear; go ahead. Now! Ticky-tick, ticky-tick – pretty to hear en, edn' 'a? And see to her fingers – tappety-tap like lightning. Nobody ever picked up the trick of it so quick as my Bess, so they tell me; but then she play the harmonium up to chapel, so her fingers are nat'rally more pliant than most. Finished, Bess? Wait a bit, then. Now you'rn there, p'raps the young fellow'd like to send another."

I thought not.

"Come now!" he expostulated. "An't there no tender young lady somewhere's, that's thinking upon 'e as anxious as your mother, and maybe a bit more so?"

I laughed and shook my head.

"Don't tell me! I'll be bound there is. And you ben't the chap to grudge sixpence to a loving maid. I'll get 'e another paper."

But this time I was firm; and fortunately at that moment

the baby created a diversion. The fair operator abandoned her instrument and rushed to soothe its cries, and I seized the opportunity to make my escape, considerably bewildered by the whole business. It is uncommon, to say the least, to find a postal official touting for orders. Mrs Dawe, coming to set lunch, deepened the mystery by shyly asking if I had sent any telegrams that morning, and by making no disguise of her satisfaction when she heard that I had.

As it happened, an unexpected matter of business sprang up, which compelled me to claim Bessie's services next morning, and at least once a day for several days after. At every visit the postmaster received me with effusive cordiality, and various hints and signs made me aware that not only he, but the entire village, regarded my telegraphic assiduity with a most favourable eye; though why this should be, I couldn't for the life of me imagine. After a week, a final telegram called me back to town; and it was then, on the eve of my departure, that a point-blank question addressed to Mrs Dawe's husband brought a solution of the mystery in a half-hour yarn, of which the following is the substance.

One spring day in the preceding year, there anchored off Port Oliver a yacht belonging to a certain wealthy and whimsical baronet, whose full name I need not mention. Let us call him Sir James. Something in the situation and appearance of the place hit his capricious fancy, and he had not been on shore half an hour before he was making inquiries about land to let. The upshot was that within a month a small army of workmen arrived and a luxurious bungalow arose as if by magic before the astonished eyes of Port Oliver. No sooner was it finished and furnished than down came Sir James and took possession; and there he remained all the summer and autumn, fishing, sailing, and entertaining the friends who came and went in a ceaseless flow.

Now Sir James was one of those who loathe letter writing, and to whom a convenient telegraph office is a necessity of life. There was nothing of the sort at Port Oliver, but Sir James was hand in glove with the rulers of this land. Mr Dawe believed there was a matter of money between them, money lent or borrowed (he wasn't sure which) to the extent of thousands of pounds. Anyhow he was in a position to bring pressure to bear on the authorities, which he did and the deficiency was remedied.

All went well for a time. Sir James and his friends sent and received their scores of telegrams weekly, and the fair Bessie became a person of importance in the village, as the depository of all manner of tasty secrets of high life. Then suddenly the volatile baronet disappeared. There were no leave-takings; he simply went off for a cruise and did not return.

Down came the workmen once more, demolished the bungalow, and carried it away piecemeal. From a hint dropped by the confidential valet who superintended the operation, Port Oliver gathered that it had probably seen the last of Sir James for ever and a day. No vestige remained of his presence, except the telegraph wire and a rubbish pit full of empty bottles, and the one was about as useful to

Port Oliver as the other; for what occasion had a quiet-living, self-contained community of fisher-folk to send telegrams? They had done very well without the wire in the past, and could do so equally well in the future.

But one day, about a week before my arrival, Jeffrey Bolitho the postmaster was much agitated and distressed – by the receipt (through the postman) of a semi-official communication from Government. Government, it seemed, was profoundly dissatisfied with the telegraphic business it had been doing of late with Port Oliver.

It complained that since Sir James's departure the messages had averaged about one a month, and the fine new wire it had put up at great expense was growing rusty for want of a proper supply of electric fluid. Moreover, in these Radical days it was as much as a Government's place was worth to continue paying a salary for a sinecure post, such as Bessie's had in fact become; and it concluded with a stony hint that, unless business brisked up immediately, it would be reluctantly compelled to pull down the posts, roll up the wire, and take the "machine" home again.

The news spread, and was received with mingled feelings. Port Oliver folk have a keen sense of their own importance, and at first the prevailing sentiment was one of indignation at what appeared to be a deliberate slight put upon the town by Government. Some ardent spirits went so far as to propose an armed demonstration with axes and the conversion there and then of the telegraph poles into firewood. But calmer counsels prevailed, and after due reflection it was candidly admitted that Government's complaint was not altogether without justification. How then was the situation to be met, with a due regard to Bessie's salary, the claims of Government, and the dignity of the town?

I will continue as nearly as possible in Mr Dawe's own words.

"Well, we talked it over, and we made up our minds to keep things going so well as we could afford to, calculating we could manage one telegram a day between us, which Bolitho reckoned 'ud be enough to keep Gov'ment quiet for a bit. So we drawed lots who should send the first, and the short straw come to me.

"Trouble was, I hadn' a notion what message to send, nor who to send it to; but at last I pitched on my brother Jack. Jack's a farmer up to Trevean in the next parish, and we hadn' seen nor heard tell of him for more 'n a month. So I thought I'd leave him know how 'twas with us, and put something beside, so's to get an answer back. So I sent this: 'All well here. What did you have for dinner today?' And I paid the reply, so's his pocket shouldn' suffer. Well, about two hours later, I got this answer: 'Fish and taties. Be you mazed?'

"Same evening, in come Jack, roving mad. You see, he was out working on the farm when the telegram came and his wife never had no such thing come to her before, and she took on dreadful, thinking somebody was dead, and not daring to open the nasty thing, as she called it. And when they'd hunted Jack up and fetched him home, there was the telegram on the table, and the missus on the floor, kicking and scritching, and all the children in a circus round her, hollering and yolling – a pretty to-do, sure 'nough.

"And things warn't much better when they found what the telegram was about. If it had been bad news, Jack's wife said she wouldn't ha' minded so much; but it put her mad to think she'd wasted a fit of asterics 'pon nothing at all, and never agin would she speak to the man that sent it, brother-in-law or none. And Jack – well, he's my brother, so no occasion to be polite, though he didn't ought to forget he's a chapel member, for all that. But when he'd gone, I said to the missus 'That's the first telegram I sent in my life, and, please-sure 'tis the last'.

"Next day was Ben Kitto's turn. Ben's a terrible Conservative, and think a brave lot of the old Queen, ever since he met her in the street one day when he was up to London, and took off his hat to her, and she bowed back to en from her carriage as polite as you please. Now some of these Radicals had been saying hard words agin her en the Sunday paper just then; so Ben thought he'd send a line just to cheer the old lady up. He's a bit of a scholar, Ben is, and long words being charged same as short, he concluded to get the best value he could for his money.

"So this was what he sent: 'Accept, obsequious assurances unmitigated loyalty.'

"But 'a didn' get no answer, though he paid for en, same as I did. And Ben haven' been the same man since. Says Royalty an't what it's cracked up to be, and he've a good mind to vote for a republic next election.

"Next was Paul Nicholls – dreadful hot man. 'Tay-kettle' we mostly do call en, being always on the boil. He had a dispute last summer with Ozias Wall the miller down to Penvose, and Ozias got the best of it, and Paul have been waiting ever since for a chance to square the yards with en. 'Now's the time, thinks he, and pitched and wrote Wall a message, hot and strong.

"Don't know what 'a was azackly, but Bolitho wouldn' take it in, said such brimstone stuff was agin regulations, and anyhow he wadn' going to allow no daughter of his to tetch en, not if 'twas only with the tips of her fingers, like. But Paul wadn' going to be put off like that, so he went off home-along and looked up a good strong text, and sent en off like this: 'See Acts Chap twenty-three beginning third verse'.

"When we come to look it up for ourselves, we found 'twas: 'Then said Paul unto him, God shall smite thee, thou whited wall' – which was uncommon conformable to the case, I think, Wall being a miller, and so floury by nature. Wall do think so too. I hear he's going about sarching for a lawyer to bring an action for scandal and vain prophesying and I reckon Paul an't so comfor'ble about it as he pretend to be.

"Then you come down and brave and thankful we've been to have'e, if 'twas only for the telegrams you've sent. 'Tis a wisht job, making bricks without straw, and I doubt we couldn' ha kept it up much longer. But now, what with those you sent and those we sent, I reckon Gov'ment have had enough to keep her quiet for the time, though I don't know what we shall do when she get hungry and begin growling agin."

I went away next morning, and have not revisited Port Oliver since. But while preparing this account, I consulted the postal guide, and was pleased to find that the little town still possesses a telegraph office; so presumably Mr Dawe and his friends managed to find some means of satisfying the appetite of Government, and preserving the credit and dignity of their native place.

St Cridda

A S YOU travel through Cornwall today, you will hardly fail to remark at the out-of-the-way situations of many of her churches. Some indeed stand, like churches elsewhere, with the homes of men clustered about them; but others are set apart on hilltops or exposed cliffs, or in sequestered inland valleys or seaward glens, where the Day of Rest is the only day of human bustle.

Of all these, none is so remote and solitary as that of St Cridda. The parish is large and wide, and contains at least one tidy village which once was a populous town. But whereas this is by the river on the northern boundary, the church hides itself in a hollow of the southern hills, with not so much as a cowshed near it. If you enquire the reason for this inconveniently retired situation, you may hear some such story as this.

When, long ago, the good bishop Jeliau and a shipload of deacons fled from the black plague that was then raging in Wales, their vessel was driven off its course by contrary winds, and put in at the harbour of the city of King Geraint. Among the company on board were St Cridda and her sister, a virgin lady named Gwenda or Gunda. Gunda was of a bilious habit, and had suffered much distress during the stormy voyage.

Having once set foot on land, she proclaimed her fixed

intention of remaining there, and would not be moved from her purpose by any arguments, sisterly or episcopal; discerning in the subversive influence of the waves a deep-laid plot of Satan to rob her of her very soul. So St Cridda, who loved her sister, gave one sigh of regret for the goodly discourse of the deacons, and cheerfully followed Gunda to land.

The ship sailed away, and the sisters set their faces inland and wandered up and down the country for many days, unprotected and unharmed. The natives were a courteous and hospitable folk, as they are to this day; and as for the giants, who still lingered here and there, waging unequal war against the saints, even they were of true Cornish blood, and raised no hand against a woman, were she saintly or sinful.

Many days they wandered, entertained now in a peasant's rude hut, now in a hermit's ruder cell, until at last they reached a spot to which no saint had hitherto penetrated, where amid laughing hills and smiling valleys a horde of untaught savages dwelt, leading gentle aimless lives.

"A fair land, sister," said St Cridda.

"Sister, a land sunk in darkness," said the virgin Gunda.

"What if we took up our abode in this fair land," said St Cridda, "and spent our days in the contemplation of God's amiable works, his laughing hills and smiling valleys, and the pretty ways of these gentle heathen? How kind they look upon us!"

For they held this discourse standing in the marketplace of a populous village, with the soft-eyed inhabitants staring in a circle about them.

"Ay, so will we," said Gunda, "and teach these poor benighted folk the blessed tidings of the wrath to come and the vengeance of the Pit. Hear how they laugh! Behold their wanton merriment in this vale of tribulation! Our mission is plain, sister. We bear the light; we will stay."

So the villagers brought clay and osiers, and built a wattled hut and thatched it with furze, and trod a hearth of hardened clay in the middle of the hut, and furnished it with two beechen stools, a water-pipkin of brown earthenware, and a heap of sweet-smelling heather for bedding; and they stocked it with jars of honey, sweet barley-leaves tinged with saffron, and a barrel of pressed pilchards, white as lilies.

And St Cridda and her sister took up their abode there, and remained many days, worshipping and doing good, each after her own fashion. Sisters they truly were, daughters both of the saintly and prolific King Brechain; but never were two of one blood less alike in appearance and disposition.

St Cridda was plump and chubby, clear-eyed and pleasant to look upon; folk turned their heads and smiled as she passed, and children encumbered the skirts of her robe. Her creed was this: that God was good, that the world was beautiful, and that the test and purpose of all doctrine was peace. She had little learning and less eloquence and of burning zeal not so much as a spark, but of love for God and His creatures a boundless store.

The virgin Gunda was tall and terrible of aspect; her flesh was wasted with indignation at the wickedness of the

177

world; her bones were eloquent through her robe of sack-cloth. Perceiving the specious beauty of evil, she thought it shameful that virtue should play the ape to vice and wear a comely garb, nor would she allow merit to those who found pleasure in good works.

In the sound of laughter she heard echoes of the convulsions of the Pit; smiles were cracks and crannies by which foul imps crept out and in; where dimples appeared, there the Evil One had set his finger. The beauty of flowers she held in suspicion; in her heart she assigned all such coloured toys and trifles to the contrivance and care of Satan. Before her eyes men walked as flaming brands, kindled from birth at the nether fires, not to be quenched without tears and ascetic practices.

Therefore she preached the gospel of mortification and earthly discomfort; her catechumens sat all day chin-deep in running water, reciting comminatory psalms; at the sight of a fair and open countenance they groaned and testified of worms; they sat on the floor at banquets and shamed the feasters with watercress and sorrel.

Gunda's eloquence was great and terrible, her zeal unbounded, her doctrine incontrovertibly implacable; yet her converts were few. The gentle heathen shrank from her talk of nether flames and tortured souls; but they gathered eagerly to hear her sister discourse of the flowery meadows of Paradise, and the good God walking there in the cool of the evening, smiling with infinite benignity at the child-angels dancing in a ring, discoursing with His saints concerning the care and management of their flock on earth, and turning aside now and again to pluck a blossom that glowed into harmless living fire at His touch.

In her secret heart Gunda despised such tame and savourless doctrine; it was a perpetual wonder and vexation to her that Cridda should be called a saint while she was denied the title.

She meditated long on this, fasting, till she thought upon a plan.

Then she went to St Cridda and said: "Look now, sister. Twelve months have I laboured among this folk, exhorting and denouncing, while you have sat at the door telling randy tales. Six souls, and six only, have I caught and caged about with terror. Their eyes are opened; as they walk, they look fearfully behind them; they shriek aloud at all seasons; they testify bravely against their wives and husbands. But what are six among such a multitude? It is time to be up and doing. Here is a flock that wanders, deaf to the shepherd, while wolves are abroad. Where is the fold to drive them into? They scatter at the sound of my voice; they hide in bushes at the sight of me approaching. They must be compelled to be persuaded.

"I cannot glaze and coax as you can. Do this for me, then: bid them bring stones and build a church, thick-walled and narrow-windowed, with a stout door and a heavy padlock thereto. Thither we will cause them to assemble, I driving, you enticing. Once within, and the door secured, they will be at our mercy. Unsparing of myself, I will exhort, denounce, inveigh, arraign, impeach, from dawn to sunset if need be. If my eloquence fails to convince, through very weariness they will surely yield, and a goodly harvest of scarified souls shall be ours. Do this, then, sister.

"The plan is mine, the work shall be mine, but you shall share the glory, even to one half."

St Cridda was gently troubled.

"Sister", she said, "to me also the thought has come, but in different guise. I have dreamt of a guest house for the good Lord to rest in when He comes this way, with pictured walls and a starry ceiling, and a carven table where He may feast with His people, and fine coloured windows and a little bell gaily jangling. But it is of a prison you speak, a dark jail for souls. Dear sister, I can have no part in such a plan."

Gunda considered, frowning.

"Be it as you will," she said at last, smiling in a politic acquiescence. But the thought in her mind was otherwise. "Once the work is begun," she thought, "who but I will be the active one, scheming, planning and directing, while she continues to sit at the door, telling her foolish tales? So the work shall be done as I desire, and the credit shall be mine also."

Then she said aloud: "As for the place of building, it is easy to choose. See there before our eyes the highest of our hills, bleak, barren and difficult of access. What more suitable spot could be found? Where could we more conspicuously affront the powers of evil that possess the land? Where could the light of our work shine more apparent? And the way to it is steep and grievous with briars and stones, as it is meet that the path of virtue should be, for the discouragement of lukewarmness and the exaltation of zeal. On the hilltop, then, we will set our church."

"Nay, sister," said St Cridda softly, "let our choice be rather some sheltered valley, a resort of God's tender creatures, where the trees will clap their hands against the windows and the blackbirds set the note to our psalms. And the way to it shall be a gentle descent, beset with flowers and turfed with sweet-smelling thyme, enticing to the feet of children and the aged."

To this Gunda would by no means agree, and began to argue the point with heat and vehemence. But St Cridda said: "Is it for us to decide? Let us await a token from our Lord. He knows."

So they rested, awaiting a sign. For in those days Nature was still the kindly mother, sedulously watching over the affairs of men, interposing at every turn to warn and direct them, showing her face to questioners in the sky, writing messages in flowers along the hedgerows, and speaking them in the voices of birds and beasts. Now she is old, a feeble grandame mumbling in the chimney corner, no one regarding what she says.

They waited, and presently they heard a discordant hallooing, and saw a loutish young giant coming towards them amusing himself, as idle lads do, by pitching two stones before him by turns as he went down the road – trying to strike one with the other. Only the stones he played with were enormous boulders; the earth quaked under their fall.

"See, sister!" cried Gunda. "See the horn'd Pagan monster! Hark to his loathsome bellowings! O that I had skill in the blessed Latin, to turn him to stone or shrivel him to a pisky's stature!"

But St Cridda arose joyfully to her feet.

"We await a sign," she said, "and here is he who shall give it."

"That lumbering limb!" exclaimed Gunda. "What manner of sign from such as he?"

"He is strong and simple," replied St Cridda. "We will bid him cast a stone in the air. Where the stone falls and rests, there will we build."

So she called out: "Pst! Pst! Come hither, little giant!"

The giant paused with a rock in his hand, and turned about and saw them, and came towards them doffing his wolfskin cap and ducking and grinning like any hobbledehoy in the presence of ladies. So St Cridda smiled back to him and bespoke him gently, praising his great strength, and begging him to make hurling-sport for their entertainment.

At the third asking he left off scratching his head and signified his willingness by leaping thrice in the air, whooping as he leapt, and tossing the great rock from hand to hand, as you might toss an apple. Then, making signs that they should follow, he led the way to a level plot of ground. Standing there he bared his arms, tossed his wolfskin cloak over his shoulder, and looked about him, deliberating in what direction he should make the cast.

Then Gunda, standing on tiptoe, secretly tugged at the

fringe of his cloak, and pointed to the high barren hill; and the giant chuckled his comprehension, and gave her to understand that the cast, though a hard one, was not beyond his powers. So he swung the stone back and forth, and taking a run, hurled it through the air. It flew high and far, till it was a pebble in their sight. Down it fell, and Gunda laughed triumphantly, seeing it strike the hilltop.

"Sister," she cried tauntingly, "what were your words? Where it falls and rests, there will we build."

"I abide by my word," said St Cridda. "Let us go to the spot."

So they went and the giant went with them keeping pace with St Cridda, as you may see a child trotting beside a pretty stranger lady in the street, unbidden and unrebuked. But when they climbed the hilltop, the stone was not there.

"I smell magic," said Gunda. "Heathen magic I smell, and spells Satanic. Else, where is the stone? What if this creature be an emissary of the Enemy, sent to mock us? Oh, that I had the Latin!"

"Patience, sister," said St Cridda. Then she turned to the giant and said gently: "Good little giant, go search."

So the giant fetched a compass about the brow of the hill, questing as he went; and presently he shouted, perceiving a great dint in the turf, where the stone had fallen; and then he hallooed at the sight of a furze-bush, all crushed and spread abroad, where it had bounced; and peering over the crest of the hill, he whistled, espying a furrow traced in the sand, where it had rolled; and shading his eyes with his hand, he hooted, pointing into the valley far below; and there, in an angle of a quiet stream, was spread the level carpet of a little meadow, and on the green carpet lay the great stone.

On that spot the church of St Cridda was built, and the stone itself was made the foundation stone; and the young giant, out of the adoring affection which he conceived for St Cridda, dedicated his mighty strength to the service of the work, with his own hands fetching from a great distance the granite blocks of which the walls were made. For this he had his reward after death, being revered on earth and welcomed in Paradise under the name of St Saxifer, which in the blessed Latin signifies "Stone-bearer".

And St Cridda, surviving him, caused to be painted on the wall of the church, over against the north door, a picture of him with the great rock poised in his hands, about to make his cast. This she did partly as a memorial, and partly to strike terror in the evil spirits who are ever thronging from their regions of polar ice to make their principal assault on the northern approaches to God's sanctuaries.

Of the virgin Gunda there is no further authentic record. In what spirit she took her disappointment, whether she humbled herself and remained to assist in the building of the church, as some believe, or whether, as others assert, she retired in a sulk to a hermitage on the top of the high barren hill, remains doubtful to this day.

For many centuries the picture remained to attest the truth of this story, until there came to the parish a foreign priest who knew or heeded nothing of the legend. Busying himself about the restoration of the church, which had fallen into decay, he caused the picture to be freshly coloured; and in place of the rock, which to him had no meaning, he ordered the painter to substitute an image of the infant Christ.

And St Saxifer, leaning over the ramparts of Paradise side by side with St Christopher, nudged his supplanter and chuckled joyously. There is no jealousy or rivalry among the saints in Paradise, but a sense of fun is not denied them.

<hr />

St Cridda may relate to the patron saint of Creed parish, the 'a' denoting a female saint. It could also be Sancreed or possibly St Credan of Bodmin.

THE STORY OF MENDU

TO CAMBALU in the days of Kublai Khan came a young man of whom a story is narrated, worthy to be written in letters of gold for the instruction and admonition of all who love the arts and practise them.

The story is wonderful in this respect, that as to its matter and application it is both sad and facetious, according to the humour of them that hear it; which is an excellent quality, and likely to be profitable to the teller. But to the teller it is neither sad nor facetious.

It is a story, told as other stories are told – for the mere pleasure of the telling, maybe, or maybe to increase the teller's fame, or maybe to fill his scanty purse; the application he leaves to his innumerable and well-born readers, who have more skill and enjoyment in such work than he. It has been well said that when the fable is written the artist pauses. It is for the world to supply the moral.

The name of the young man was Mendu, and in the beginning he was a goat herd on the plains of Tartary. Men say that these plains are the roof of the world, fashioned last of all by the gods, when their hands were cramped with toil and they had grown weary of their task.

So the plains are negligently constructed of inferior material, of barren rocks and shifting sand, and there were no trees left in the storehouse of the gods to plant therein

– no, not even a shrub, nothing but scanty grass and bitter herbs.

Over the plains hovered countless eagles and hawks of the rock. But the singing-birds, the gentle and delicate ones, shunned them, finding no eligible trees or commodious bushes to build their nests in. And the ears of the gods, insatiate of praise, were distressed, for it is an axiom current in the courts of the gods, that where no music is, there is no worship. And it is their comfortable doctrine that he who sings, thereby does the gods homage whether he will or no.

Therefore, to save the land from the consequences of impiety, the gods endowed its rude and unpolished inhabitants with the gift of song in superabundant measure. No voices were so sweet as theirs, no fingers so skilful in the manipulation of all kinds of musical instruments. Day and night an unbroken thread of melody was spun over those desolate plains. From sheep-walk to goat-pasture it stretched, a link between herdsman and herdsman, so that solitude was not in that most solitary of lands. The gods, to whom sound is a visible thing, coloured brightly or dully according to its melodiousness or harshness, looked down and beheld a golden web spread on the earth's housetop, glittering in the sun, glimmering in the moon – a lovely sight.

Such was the birthplace of Mendu. At his mother's breast he drank in melody, and the feet of his soul were firm on the heaven-scaling ladder of notes ere yet he had learnt the terrestrial art of walking.

As he grew up he acquired the knowledge of all musical instruments that were known in the land, to whit, the goat-skin pipes, the flageolet, the sheep's-horn trumpet and the five various kinds of lute. His aptitude was marvellous, and even in that land of musicians there was none to excel him. And as he sat on the rocks, wrapped in his cloak, the herds wandering about him, he had but to gaze skywards, abstracting his eyes from the contemplation of earthly things, and all the host of lovely sounds came fluttering down, stately, gay and languorous, before him. Then he would seize an appropriate instrument, a lute, pipe, trumpet or flageolet, and translate those spiritual dances into sensuous melody.

And thereupon the neighbouring shepherds would cease from their piping and listen until he made an end, when they too would catch at the melody and repeat it, and others beyond would hear them and do the same, and beyond them yet others. Like the waters of a fountain that suddenly bubble up through the sand and spread over the plain, so the music made by Mendu spread from the rock he sat on over the length and breadth of Tartary. His fame was great. Happy, too, was his lot – for a while. So long as he took no heed of his fame, but remained content with the cave of his flocks and the solitary exercise of his divine gift, so long was he happy.

But it chanced that one evening he made a new ditty out of contemplation of the sunset. In delicate correspondence with the shifting, melting hues of the western sky he composed it, and played it on his flageolet. Twice he played it, and took the reed from his lips, and sat in a calm ecstasy, watching the light fade and the stars appear. And the uncertain breezes that wander about the plains at twilight brought to his ears diverse echoes of the ditty from the pipes of other shepherds, some near, some afar off.

Then Mendu felt an agreeable tickling at the roots of his heart, and he fell into a meditation, saying to himself: "Certainly my musical skill is not to be despised, seeing that others, skilled ones also, are content to imitate me."

The thought was new to him, and he pondered upon it, till that which tickled his heart grew insistent, and began to prick. And again he said: "Assuredly my power is great over the hearts of men. When I am gay, they are gay also, and when I choose to be soberly contemplative, they are unanimous in sobriety of contemplation. This a wonderful thing, and unheard of."

So he meditated on the wonderful thing, and the pricking grew painful in its intensity. And once more he said: "The fact of my greatness is undeniable. It is a marvel that it should have escaped me hitherto. Yet what stranger would guess it, observing my condition? Is the tending of ignoble and malodorous goats a fit occupation for genius – or a faded robe of undyed goatskin suitable apparel, or goat's milk adequate nourishment for the same? Truly there is injustice here."

He brooded on the injustice, and it was as if the needles that pricked his heart were being heated to a red heat, searing him and goading him towards he knew not what.

And yet again he said: "Evil is my fate. For long have I

been the most unfortunate of young men, and knew it not. Great are the privileges of genius – fame, popular adulation, fine wines, dainty dishes, all these and more. And here I sit in rags on a rock of irksome angularity, tending mangy cattle."

And he was moved to tears by the sorry contrast, and at the thought of the years he had wasted in ignorant happiness. And the miracle of genius was accomplished in him. For while the man wept, the artist stood aloof, contemplating the woeful spectacle, and found it of vast interest and fit to be turned to account. So while yet he sobbed, he said to himself: "Surely here is excellent material for song. I will melodize my woe."

Setting down the flageolet, he took up a lute of five strings, and played thereon a lugubrious prelude, and sang of the nothingness of things, the pathos of unrecognised genius, the disgusting sourness of goat's milk, and other kindred themes. And when he had exhausted the emptiness of the universe, he paused and listened eagerly.

And in the deep silence of the night he heard the voices of the neighbouring shepherds essaying to reproduce the melody of his song. But their attempts were hesitating and broken, with many incorrect interpolations, like the speech of foreigners in a strange country, the language of which is unknown to them and difficult on their tongues.

And long before the end was attained they broke down and ceased abruptly.

And the gods, peering earthwards, were amazed to see a blood-red spot appear and wax in the centre of the golden web, while the threads about it quivered violently and were snapped.

At first Mendu was cast down, and lamented grievously, saying: "Now even that small modicum of popularity I possessed is snatched from me, because I refuse to pander to the facile optimism of the vulgar herd, but heroically follow the bent of my retired and melancholy genius."

But on reflection he was comforted even to elation, exclaiming: "See now, even my brethren in art understand me not! Now there can be no doubt of my exceeding greatness. My light dazzles their weak eyes. They are in darkness because of its splendour."

Throughout the night he sat sleepless, while cloaked assailants crept up in the darkness and hammered at the door of his heart, and the inmates thereof alternately cowered in pale despondency and burned with the resolve of a hazardous sally.

When day dawned, he turned his face towards the east. Its swelling pomp of gold and scarlet burst upon him like a flourish of summoning trumpets, and he leapt to his feet, crying: "It is resolved! Two curses are on this land – superfluity of talent and deficiency of wealth.

Because of these my genius is unmarked and unrewarded. I will leave these barren wastes and descend into Cathay, that region of great cities. In every street of the cities are golden palaces, where idle rich men sit, impatiently awaiting the advent of genius, that they may honour and reward it.

There are also magnificent cook-shops in the streets,

already their delectable odours mount to my soul, inspiring me. I will depart without delay."

So he gathered up his various musical instruments, his pipes, flageolet, trumpet and lutes, and slung them in convenient positions about his person, and tightened his sandals and stepped out bravely in the direction of the rising sun, singing as he went.

Long and far he wandered, and came to many cities, but made no stay in any, because they were abodes unsuitable for genius, their palaces being of stone merely, their cookshops musty, unclean, without architectural pretensions.

At last, when the leather of his sandals was dust in the road behind him, and only the strings remained, he arrived at Cambalu, where the Great Khan was wont to hold his court in winter. His heart leapt, for the cook-shops of Cambalu were palaces, its palaces abodes for the gods. From every window came the sound of music, and at this also he rejoiced, perceiving its inferior quality. At every discord he smiled, from every harsh note he drew a happy augury.

"My day has dawned!" he exclaimed. "Already the sun of my destiny mounts high in the heavens." And he varied the application of the metaphor, saying: "Lo, a city benighted, painfully groping after the suspected treasures of Art, kindling feeble rush-lights, stumbling up blind alleys. Great its joy and gratitude when the sun rises and the jewel of its desire is revealed."

Then he debated in what favoured spot, to what favoured audience the revelation should be made, and he resolved to demand admission to the presence of the Khan himself, no other. So he inquired his way to the Khan's palace, and approached the door of the hall of audience. As he came near, the keeper of the door observed him, and called out in the monotonous voice of one who repeats a set formula: "The right of entry is withheld from wandering beggars."

And Mendu answered hotly: "Thou rude fellow without culture, I am no wandering beggar, but a musician of genius. In the sacred name of Art I demand admittance."

"The invocation is ineffective, seeing that I am a rude fellow without culture," said the other, and closed the door.

Then Mendu shook the dust of the palace court from his feet and departed, prophesying disaster to the Kingdom through the iniquitous imbecility of the Khan's doorkeeper. As it is written: When the gate hangs awry, the house is near its fall. And next he turned his steps to the golden palaces where the dukes and nobles dwelt, but the proud lackeys repulsed him with contumely, discourteously animadverting on the doubtful cleanliness of his person, accusing him of harbouring guests with whom their masters desired no acquaintance.

From door to door he went, and found no welcome, till candid confidence melted to red rage within him, and red rage was chilled to black despair. At last he said: "My error is gross and obvious. It becomes not the dignity of genius to fawn upon the rich, the ignorantly purse-proud. The patronage of kings and nobles is a doubtful favour, humiliating, insecure; their taste in art is notoriously questionable. But the great heart of the people beats warmly and truly. Once gained, it is a safe possession for ever. I will go forth and perform in the streets."

So he betook himself to the market-place, and unslinging his pipes, played a selection of the choicest and merriest airs he had made while he was yet a happy goat herd. For it is to be noted that inspiration had unaccountably deserted him since he left the plains of Tartary; in vain he lifted his eyes to these new heavens; no lovely bevy of sounds descended from them as heretofore. And while he played a great crowd gathered about him.

But as soon as he ceased it melted with miraculous swiftness, with intent to avoid the customary and unseasonable appeal to its pockets. Seeing this, Mendu clutched in dismay at the garments of several, crying: "I am Mendu, a musician of genius, from Tartary I come. What think ye of my music?"

"It is sadly uncouth and rustical," they replied. "And the fashion of it is old. It is also displeasing by reason of its frivolous vivacity. Know, O stranger, that the modern taste is all for the chromatic wailings of intense passion and the monotonous moans of settled melancholy. Naught else captivates our ears. These six months we have found pleasure only in sadness, and no sadness is discoverable in your obvious rhythms and your themes of vulgar simplicity. Loose your hold from our garments, O stranger, accepting from us a solemn assurance of the emptiness of our purses."

So they departed, leaving Mendu aquiver with rage and

disappointment. He rushed blindly forth from the market-place and hurried along many streets, taking no heed of his whereabouts.

When he came to himself he stood before a great building of unfamiliar aspect, and enquiring, learned that it was the college of the Khan's imperial musicians.

"There is a destiny in this," he said joyfully. "All unknowing I have been guided to my brothers in Art at the time when most of all I crave for brotherly sympathy and succour. The building is magnificent – a fit setting for the consummate pearl of genius. I will enter and claim admission into the ranks of the imperial musicians. Surely, if merit avails, I shall be set among the chiefs. Then will the people bow to me in the market-place, and the nobles practise deference, and the Khan's rascally door-keeper be confounded."

So he knocked, and demanded speech with the chief musicians; and being brought into their presence, he recited his qualifications and proffered his request, recounting also the scandalous rebuffs he had lately endured.

Khadu Khan, chief among the chiefs, replied: "This is the abode of generosity and virtue; none can accuse us of turning our backs on approved merit. But first it must be approved. An examination is necessary, and a trial of skill."

"Willingly I submit to the trial," exclaimed Mendu; and already his fingers were plucking at the strings of his lute, when Khadu Khan lifted a restraining hand.

"Nay," he said. "First a preliminary formality, repugnant to our generous natures, but enjoined by law, and therefore to be complied with, however reluctantly. It is this – the payment, in advance, of a trifling fee."

At these words apprehension stiffened Mendu's fingers on the strings, and he asked timidly: "The amount?"

"The amount," said Khadu Khan, "is benevolently proportioned to the means of the candidate, who is required to exhibit the contents of his purse."

Hearing this, Mendu slowly extracted from the folds of his garment a purse of exiguous dimensions, and emptied it before the chief musicians. One gold sequin it contained, and one silver diner, no more.

"Account thyself fortunate," said Khadu Khan, "for the sum is the smallest that the unalterable laws of our corporation permit us to accept." And as the coins disappeared within his voluminous robes, he added: "Let the trial commence."

So Mendu swept the chords of his lute and played the composition he knew to be his best. The Symphony of Love and Destiny was its title. At the commencement was heard an amorous theme, broken, faltering, expressive of the birth of youthful affection; presently it changed its character and flowed with a gentle confidence, fathering force and volume, until suddenly it burst forth into the full tide of overwhelming rapture. And as one listened, one was gradually aware of a certain subdued but persistent muttering of sombre import in the lower chords of the instrument.

Slowly it arose, and did battle with the other, until the two were confounded in terrible discord. And the amorous

197

air grew faint and sank before its stern adversary, but only for a while; soon a new spirit was infused into it, and avoiding further struggle, it soared and floated triumphant among the highest strings. In vain the other attempted to follow; thrice it clambered up and fell back groaning; then its rancour subsided, its spirit was broken, and in the end it was heard tinkling a submissive accompaniment to the paean of Love victorious. For this was the meaning of the symphony, that by loftiness of aspiration Love may conquer even Fate, master of all beside.

Full of high confidence was Mendu when he dropped his lute and awaited the verdict of the musicians. And full of grave reprobation were the faces they turned upon him.

Said one: "I heard the first note only; it was an illegal discord; I stopped my ears."

Said another: "Watching carefully, I observed this person making use of his thumb to stop the frets with; which thing is justly forbidden by law, the thumb being an ignoble member, of clumsy, dwarfish stature, unfit for such divine and perfect services."

Said a third: "What saith Mencius? The sole end of music is the inculcating of filial piety. I find no observation of this maxim here; wherefore I suspect this person of being a base parricide, in intention if not in deed."

A fourth said: "It is new – evil therefore." A fifth: "It is old – a maladroit plagiarism from the works of antique masters." A sixth: "It is mere cacophony – the meaningless ravings of a frenzied maniac." A seventh: "Nay, it hides a deep meaning, and a criminal; in certain combinations of notes I have discovered subtle incentives to treason against the Khan our master."

Then Khadu Khan bent his brows sternly on Mendu, and said: "Behold the unanimity of my brethren; with one voice they condemn thee; I also. Depart therefore, thou law-breaker, parricide, innovator, plagiarist, madman, and crafty rebel, lest we summon the city guard and have thee cast into prison."

Woeful was the visage of Mendu; his palsied astonishment laughable to behold. For a while he stood speechless; then with a lamentable voice he cried: "At least return to me my monies, that I may not starve in this inhospitable city."

"The list of thy crimes is already long," said Khadu Khan. "Now another is added to them – the crime of attempted extortion. Begone, thou thief, thou blackmailer! Thy impudent demands avail nothing against our sublime inerrability."

Then Mendu rushed forth, beating his breast and shouting invectives against Cambalu and all its inhabitants. Alone, penniless, in a strange land – truly his condition was a sorry one. Hunger gnawed him; the profusion of cook-shops was a source of torment to him as he wandered through the streets. Two days he wandered, eating his soul out in default of grosser nourishment. On the third day his legs failed him suddenly in the market-place, and he sank on the ground, faint and weary unto death. And there, with the bustle of sleek citizens about him, he philosophised gloomily on his condition.

"Now," he said, "I perceive the true nature of genius, and the reason why the gods hold it in abhorrence and persecute it. It fits not into their scheme; nor is it of their making, but another's. When they made the universe, it was after the fashion of a machine, a great praying-wheel, the earth its axle, the stars the shining nails that stud its circumference. With a twirl of the hand they set it spinning, and lolled back in their seats, listening complacently to the hum thereof. Without worship they perish; it is their sole nourishment. Therefore they formed the universe like a praying-wheel, and ordained that it should spin for ever.

"But that which is beyond the gods was displeased at their greedy vanity, and took two handfuls of sand and small pebbles and began to drop them slowly into the machine, impeding the motion thereof. Grain by grain the sand trickled through the fingers of that Nameless One, while the gods squirmed uneasily on their cushions, foreseeing the end. Their torture is prolonged; still the sand trickles, and I am one of the grains thereof; my fate, to be ground to dust in the axle.

"And what is the contumely that assails genius but the protesting squeal of the machine as it revolves over the foreign obstacle, crushing it? To be the last, the arresting grain, to perish achieving the final defeat of the gods – that were a noble fate. But I – I fall to dust, and still the wheel revolves, nor is its velocity perceptibly diminished. To dust I fall, sooner or later; and soon or late, what matters it to a worthless grain of sand?"

He stared up into the sky, absorbed in dismal meditation. Long he lay there, unable to stir by reason of his increasing weakness, while the merchants chaffered about him, and the porters, hurrying to and fro with their loads, cursed as they stumbled over his body. And as he lay, gazing heavenwards, lo, a wonder!

To his eyes, purged of the film of conceit by suffering and the approach of death, was vouchsafed yet again the vision of sweet sounds – not coming, as aforetime, garlanded, gaily clad, treading light measures, but solemnly pacing the air in robes of sober magnificence, bearing white poppies in their hands.

And Mendu smiled radiantly, and his miserable condition became as nothing to him; nothing to him the world of gods and men; all faded, as ugly phantoms fade at daybreak.

He collected his strength and staggered to his feet, saying: "Once more; claiming no merit, teaching nothing; neither selfishly nor unselfishly; not for my own pleasure nor yet for the pleasure of others; but for the sake of Beauty, which is beautiful without reason and without reward."

He took his lute and played. And as he played the buyers and sellers ceased from bargaining and gathered about him, listening in hushed wonder. Never before had they heard such music; nor could they fit a meaning to it; it was like the spell of a sorcerer that compels obedience though uttered in a strange tongue. In their hundreds they gathered about Mendu; but he saw them not, nor heeded them, smiling upwards. And as he finished he fell dead.

Then there was a great commotion; and they questioned one another, saying: "Who was this man?"

And some came forward and said: "We had speech with him lately. Mendu his name, a musician from Tartary."

Then the name of Mendu was buzzed about, he lying dead. And people said: "How pathetic his fate! How thrillingly dramatic!" And they gloated on the circumstances, and shouldered one another about the body, shivering pleasurably. And they said further: "O untimely lot, thus to be cut down on the threshold of fame! One minute longer, and we had acclaimed him a master of song. His music was wonderful, full of delectable melancholy, haunting the ear with a sweet persistence. Let us consider; how went it?"

"Thus," said one, humming a phrase.

"Not so, but thus," said another, correcting him.

And a third said: "Nay, my brothers; the length of your ears is out of all proportion to their acuteness. Listen, it was thus."

Then they wrangled together, disputing each bar, mingling abuse with fragmentary melodic illustrations. Great was the uproar and disturbance over Mendu's song; he lying dead.

And coming to no agreement, they separated in anger and went their ways, each humming his own version. And the noise of the occurrence spread over the city; men talked of nothing else, nor would they listen to any music but the death-song of Mendu.

Anarchy reigned in Cambalu, because of the disparity of

the different versions; friends came to blows over a discord, and brothers were divided by a semitone.

Soon the matter came to the ears of the Khan, who sent for his chief musicians and ordered them to restore harmony in the province of sounds. So the chiefs appointed commissioners to go forth into the city and recover the true version.

They returned, and behold, versions a thousand and one, all different, all authentically reported by ear-witnesses. So the chiefs received the documents and sat on them in committee. Many months they sat on them, and hatched a voluminous book, voluminously entitled – The Art of the Great Mendu, Critically Considered in its Relations to Arithmetic, Morals, and Music; together with an Accurate Text of his Sole Remaining Work, Carefully Collated from Oral Traditions, with Conjectural Emendations and Additions by the Members of the Imperial College of Cathayen Musicians. To which is Subjoined a Proposal for the Erection of a Fitting Memorial to the Deceased Artist.

And in the book tactful reference was made to Mendu's examination before the board of the college; regret was expressed that certain abstruse technicalities had rendered his rejection unavoidable; his intemperate behaviour on that occasion was lightly and leniently animadverted upon; and that full and generous forgiveness was accorded him, which is the happy privilege of the dead.

And with regard to the text of the Death-Song, much praise was due to the imperial musicians for their tender and reverent treatment of it, purging it of the faults and extravagances of untaught and ill-regulated genius, and polishing and smoothing its all too vigorous phrases down to a decent and agreeable flatness. And furthermore since the enduring fame of their illustrious dead is an object of great solicitude to the Cathayans, greater even than the prosperity of their illustrious living, the imperial musicians proposed that a new School of Music should be founded, to be called after Mendu's name; the study of his work to be carried on therein. And to this end they solicited subscriptions from all lovers of Art.

Then the nobles brought their gold, the merchants their silver, the common people their strings of copper cash; for the memory of Mendu was dear to them, because of the tear-compelling pathos of his death and the titillating mystery that surrounded his life. And the School of Mendu was established and affiliated to the Imperial College; and certain necessitous members of the college were appointed with fat salaries to conduct the school. Once a year they lectured on the great Mendu of pious memory; the rest of the time, that they might not remain idle, they expounded each his own private doctrines of art to the students.

So that Glory, which the poet has declared to be the sunshine of the dead, poured its rays on Mendu as he wandered down the black gulf.

But it is to be doubted if his lean and shivering ghost got much warmth or comfort thereby.

Portrait Of A Cornish Musician

———◆◦◆———

I T IS NOW more than fifty years since our church
orchestra was abolished, but affectionate memories of
the "musicianers" and their ways survive in plenty
among the older folk of the parish. The band, consisting of
two flutes, two clarinets and two bass-viols, sat in the front
of the old west gallery – long since chopped down – with
the choir of men and boys grouped about them.

As soon as the psalm was given out, one of the bass-viols
proclaimed the key by scraping the four notes of the common chord from top to bottom, and away went players and
singers in full cry through the allotted verses of Tate and
Brady to Dowland's Old Common or Ravenscroft's
Salisbury, or some other ancient and dignified tune out of
Hullah's Psalter. When a clarinet "cowked" or made the
harsh sound incident to reed instruments when moisture
fails them, the player would stamp down the gallery, go
outside, and dip his reed in the stream that flowed past the
churchyard gate.

They were an independent crew, impatient of outside
interference in the choice and conduct of psalm or anthem,
and recognising no distinction of creed in matters pertain-
ing to their art. The old manor house adjoining the church

was occupied by a community of Carmelite nuns, and public service was performed in their chapel every Sunday morning at ten o'clock.

The musicians, some of whom belonged to the English and some to the Roman Church, used first to attend and play at the celebration of Mass, and then they would slip across and take their places in time for eleven o'clock service. There were some quaint characters among them; of one in particular a most curious and engaging portrait is preserved in the memories of those who knew him.

He played one of the bass-viols, and he first took his seat in the gallery when he was still too small to carry his unwieldy instrument to church without assistance. In maturer years his performance was especially distinguished by its vigour.

When playing at merry-making he would regularly wear his bowstring through in the course of the evening. People can recall the quick impatient gesture with which he would strip off the loosened hairs from time to time. In later years, after the disbandment of the orchestra, he took up the harmonium, which he played with great expression, but also with such exceeding deliberation that it required a strong mental effort to follow him; though, if the hearer's mind could only carry on the theme from one long-drawn chord past the lengthy pause to the next long-drawn chord, the performance was enjoyable in its linked sweetness.

There is a pretty picture of him as an old man, seated at the harmonium and playing and humming the Qui Tollis from a Mozart Mass, the tears streaming down his cheeks the while. Good music, he said, always made him feel sorrowful. He was a plasterer and paperhanger by trade; they say he was apt to be lazy and negligent over his work unless the job appealed to him by calling for a touch of artistry.

When he got past work he subsisted on a pittance allowed him by a well-to-do relative, living an odd kind of hermit life in a tumble-down thatched cottage set in the middle of an orchard.

His poverty was not to be made a show of, and nobody was allowed inside the cottage; the door was kept locked whether he was in or out, and all the windows were boarded up. He rose at two in the morning, sat down to dinner at the sound of the nine o'clock school-bell, and went to bed at other folks' tea-time. His harmonium was placed in the attic, and he made an opening in the thatch above it, for he liked to have the blue sky over him when he played.

Once some inquisitive boys climbed up on the roof and tried to peep down through the hole, but he marked their purpose and frustrated it with an open umbrella. Like the birds, he considered the fresh hours of the morning to be the most appropriate for music; in summer he would often be playing at dawn, when only he and the thrushes were awake.

He was a Roman Catholic, and his piety was profound and profuse. It was his innocent boast that he said more prayers than any other man in the parish, his custom being to "pitch praying", as he expressed it, as soon as he awoke, and to continue the exercise for an hour before getting up.

He had a few amiable weaknesses. One was for fine clothes; and as his benefactor kept him liberally supplied with cast-off garments, he was able to indulge his passion to an inordinate extent, as some might think; it being his habit after working hours to don two complete suits, one over the other, supplementing them in winter with a third pair of trousers and an overcoat or two.

A touch of personal vanity was excusable, as he was a singularly handsome old man, with fine-cut features and a venerable white beard. A child who was taken to chapel one day when he happened to be serving Mass, came home enraptured at having at last seen Father Christmas in the flesh.

He also loved good ale, a little too well. People in whose houses he was working found it prudent to deny his requests for liquor until the job was done; for a pint was enough to make him drowsy, and he would then watch his opportunity, slip upstairs into a bedroom, push the bed up against the door, and fall into a slumber from which no knocking or shouting could arouse him.

In later years, credit was opened for him to the extent of one daily glass of beer at the village inn and at two others, a mile or two away in opposite directions, and in spite of steep hills and rheumatic pains he generally contrived to keep the account clear at all three until the day when he took to his bed.

When the end was near, he called for the girl who led the church choir, and asked her to sing over the grave at his funeral, not that he would be there to hear her, even in the spirit – by that time he would be "sitting alongside of mother, playing the bass-viol". But it was his desire that his stay on earth should be rounded off with sweet sounds.

Mawgan Church Town

NICK: Kind friends will you give me your careful attention, I've come here this evening to sing a new song!

SAM: If you ask me what I'm doing here, perhaps I may mention, I've come just to help the poor fella along – but what is your subject?

NICK: My subject's a fine one the best you will find if you search up and down; I'll tell you directly.

SAM: Well come now what is it?

NICK: It's Mawgan!

SAM: What? Mawgan?

NICK: Yes Mawgan Church Town.

BOTH: You may search in and out, you may search up and down, but you won't find an equal to Mawgan Church Town, Trevarrian, Tregurrian, Trevenna, Carloggas, Trenoon and Bolingey and Mawgan Church Town.

NICK: Now Mawgan is famous all over the nation.

SAM: There isn't a place can with Mawgan compare.

NICK: For men that are handsome.

SAM: And maids that are fair,

NICK: Of handsome young chaps – you've a sample before you, of sweet young maidens we grow a fine crop.

SAM: But if you're requiring the pick of the market, don't waste time up yonder – come over to shop.

BOTH: You may search in and out, down below and up top, but the pick of the bunch you'll find over to shop, oh! The Lobbs and Beswethericks and Richards' and Charles' and Granny Trebilcock, all over to shop.

SAM: I hear that the Railway is coming to Mawgan!
NICK: Ah! What will St Columb folk say about that?
SAM: And as soon as it comes we shall all make our fortunes.
NICK: With nothing to do but sit still and grow fat.
SAM: And the strangers will come in their scores and their hundreds, from East and from West; and from South and from North.
NICK: There'll be 15 hotels, each as big as the Headland!
SAM: And a street of fine houses from Winsor to Porth!
BOTH: Oh won't it be grand when the railway comes down, we shan't know ourselves up to Mawgan Church Town, St Columb and Newquay and Truro and Plymouth, will take a back seat to Mawgan Church Town.

SAM: We've a choir down to Mawgan!
NICK: I'm in it.
SAM: And I too.
NICK: And I take the principal tenor.
SAM: (You try to) and I lead the basses.
NICK: (Oh get along). And not long ago we enjoyed a fine supper, with jellies and junkets and gallons of craim, but the very next day we all had –
SAM: Influenza! At least we thought better to call it that same.

BOTH: You may search in and out – you may hunt up and down, but you'll find no such choir as at Mawgan Church Town, there's Sam and there's Nick, there's Ern and there's Dick, all in the choir of Mawgan Church Town.

NICK: I don't like to say there are rogues down to Mawgan.
SAM: But if there are any they better take care.
NICK: For our policeman is training a terrible bloodhound, to track every criminal down to his lair, now our policeman's abroad at all times and all seasons, when you meet him out late, you may think he's alone, but he isn't!
SAM: The bloodhound's inside his fob pocket, all ready to spring when the whistle is blown.
BOTH: So you wreckers take care and you poachers look out, there's a terrible, horrible bloodhound about, he'll catch you and snatch you and nip you and grip you, and tear you to pieces before you can shout.

SAM: Last night we went up to the shop for some bacca, Miss Houghton called 'Emma', they searched all around.
NICK: They searched in the parlour, they searched in the oven, but nowhere at all could that bacca be found.
SAM: They searched in the flour bag and under the counter, they searched over stairs and they searched in the yard.
NICK: It was past 2am when they found that tobacco, up chimney along with the muslin and lard!
BOTH: You may search in and out, down below and up top, but nowhere you'll find such a wonderful shop, there's but-

211

ter and bonnets, and chiffons and codfish, all mixed up together in the one little shop.

SAM: And now we have come to the end of our ditty.

NICK: Well our ditty can't go on for ever that's plain, but isn't there time for a slap at the Parson?

SAM: Ssh I see him down yonder – we better refrain, the hour's getting late, it's time to give over – to take up the platform and turn the lights down.

NICK: Our concert is over, but if you've enjoyed it, we'll soon have another in Mawgan Church Town.

BOTH: You may search in and out, you may hunt up and down, but you won't find an equal to Mawgan Church Town, Lanvean and Polgreen and Tolcarne and Trevedras, Lanherne and Nanskeval and Gluvian and Deerpark, Trenance and Retallick, Denzell and Moreland, Trevarrian, Tregurrian, Trenoon and Carloggas, Trevenna, Bolingey and Mawgan Church Town!

– AS SUNG BY SAM AND NICK LOBB

BALDHEAD

A LETTER to Olive: Thursday. Some sunshine this morning. On the common after breakfast. This will be a record year for berries. The small boys are already about with ladders after the blackberries and I never saw such a show of hawthorn "aglets". Robins singing fiercely against one another in the hawthorn wood. I have to record a singular adventure that happened to me as I was sitting under the willow. It was quite still at first, but presently a gentle air began to stir, and I was aware of a multitude of confused little voices overhead. To begin with, I could distinguish nothing, but soon the voices took order in a regular chorus, and I could clearly make out a united cry of "Baldhead! Baldhead!" I looked up and at once the agitation among the leaves increased, and this is what I heard:

THEM: Baldhead, Baldhead, tell us true,
Where's the darksome girl in blue?
ME: What the devil's that to you?
THEM: Grumpy Baldhead, Baldhead rude,
Sitting there in solitude,
What's become of Pussy-kitten?
Has she given you the mitten?
Day by day you sit alone,

(Ssh! We heard it! Heard him groan!)
Sit alone and grow no fatter,
Tell us, Baldhead, what's the matter?
ME: Can't you stop your silly chatter?
THEM: (Poor old Baldhead! How he grieves.
Twenty thousand little leaves,
All with sympathy a-flutter
At the groan we heard him utter!)
Dear old Baldhead, don't be bitter,
See us flutter, hear us twitter,
With anxiety astir
Lest some harm has come to her,
Her the lithesome girl in blue,
Tell us quick and tell us true,
Ere we turn from green to yellow,
Has she found another fellow?
(There, there, you needn't bellow)
Is she sitting on his knees
Down beside the Cornish seas?
Does she drink his love outpoured
Through the streets of Camelford?
Do they wander hand in hand
Over fair Trebarwith Strand?
Do they clamber, brisk and agile
O'er the rocks of famed Tintagel?
Seek communion, soul with soul,
'Mid the slates of Delabole?
Does he promise to be true
To his winsome girl in blue?

Does he bring, to prove his word,
Chocolates you can't afford?
Or to fill with bliss her chalice,
Take her to a picture palace?
By permission of her Mamma,
There to see a Cowboy Dramma?
How it thrills her through and through,
Sentimental girl in blue.
How she clutches at his arm
When the hero comes to harm.
How the happy teardrops flow
When the villain is laid low.
Hear her, when the show is over,
Sweetly thank her generous lover.
Hear her vote a horrid bore
All that made life sweet before:
'Poets new and poets old,
After this, you leave me cold,
Johnny Keats and Rupert Brooke,
Ella Wilcox, 'Lisa Cooke,
Flecker, Davies, De la Mare,
Yours is unsubstantial fare,
Words, words, words, as light as air.
Give me for my satisfaction,
Action, action, action, action!
Trains colliding, bombs a-busting,
Swords and daggers cut and thrusting.
Penny plain may suit the dull herd,
I prefer the tuppence coloured.'

Poor old Baldhead, give it up.
Hold your nose and drain the cup.
Darksome winsome girls in blue
Are not for likes of you.
Who the paths of love would fare on
First must learn to keep his hair on.
Be contented with your lot,
Wear a wig and be forgot.

But here I lost patience and got up and went away, pursued for some distance by a tiny multitudinous shout of "Baldhead! Baldhead!" Of course I admit that, seen from above in perspective, my tonsure may appear rather extensive; but all the same, to draw attention to it in such a marked fashion is nothing but impertinence in a pack of leaves not six months old.

<hr />

Olive was Charles Lee's second wife. She was several years his junior and these romantic, self-effacing lines were written from Letchworth before they were married, and while she was in Gorran.

THE STUFFED OWL
– A PROEM

Bad Verse I sing, and since 'twere best, I deem
'I' employ a style that suits my swelling theme,
First, in my lines some flatulence t' infuse,
I thus invoke the Muddle-headed Muse,
Ascent, O CACHOHYMNIA, from the deep,
Where BLACKMORE mumbles epics in his sleep,
While by a mud-pool endless Birthday Odes
CIBBER recites, and charms the list'ning toads;
What time his placid Pegasean steed,
Browsing along th' adjacent thistly mead,
Pricks his tall ears, and lengthens out his bray
In faithful echo of his master's lay.
Adjust thy wig, eternally awry,
And wipe the gummy rheum from either eye.
Endeavour not (vain task) to tune thy lyre,
Nor stay to renovate that rusty wire;
For in thy strain should any note be missing,
Thy sacred bird's at hand to fill the gap with hissing.
She comes! She comes! Like castanets of Spain,
Clip-clop, clip-clop, her slippers, strike the plain,
While from her lips proceeds th' oracular hum:
"De-dum, de-dum, de-dumty, dum de-dum."

217

A gander limps with outstretch'd neck before her,
And owls and jays and cuckoos hover o'er her.
Brisk at her elbow NAMBY PAMBY skips,
Checking her chant on quiv'ring finger-tips;
And close behind, strutting in laurell'd state,
See! AUSTIN arm-in-arm with PYE and TATE.
Follows a crowd confus'd of wigs and hats:
HAYLEYS and BAYLYS, JERNINGHAMS and
SPRATS;
A horde of DELLA CRUSCANS, chanting, panting,
Thrilling and shrilling, canting and re-canting;
Bristolia's biblipolic bard, JOE COTTLE,
Hugging four epics – and a blacking-bottle;
T. BAKER, who Steam's gospel best delivers;
The Reverend WHUR, and Georgia's pride, DOC
CHIVERS;
And ELLA, who from ev'ry pore exudes
Impassion'd transatlantic platitudes.
And who comes now, hee-hawing down the wind?
'Tis Colley's Pegasus! And these, entwin'd
In amorous embrace upon his crupper?
ELIZA COOK and MARTIN FARQUHAR TUPPER!
Now the cortege, advancing, nears the spot
Where rubbish from Parnassus hill is shot.
Here batter'd tropes and similes abound,
And metaphors lie mix'd in many a mound
And oily rags of sentiment bestrew the ground.
With shouts exultant, see th' excited troop
Rush on the spoil, and grab and grub and scoop,

And snatch and scuffle. With indulgent mien,
Awhile the muse surveys the busy scene;
A tow'ring Gradus-heap she then ascends,
And, hawking thrice, the toil below suspends.
Her scholars, in a nudging, shuffling line,
Attend the utt'rance of the voice divine.
Like schoolboys of fourteen her accents thrill,
Now rumbling deep, now stridulating shrill;
And these her words, transcrib'd by my unworthy quill:
"Not without dust and heat are prizes won.
Hot, dusty ones, your Muse applauds: well done!
Some words of counsel now, ere you disperse,
Your swag to file and flatten into verse.
"Let others vie, as PINDAR vied before,
With eagles that monotonously soar;
The various-gifted dabchick be your model,
Skilful to splash, and flap, and wade, and waddle,
And in that art which none achieve by thinking,
Skilfull'st of all – I mean the Art of Sinking.
"Not that I bid you never rise at all,
Or shun th' eclat that greets a sudden fall.
So, when in yard suburban we survey
The high-stretch'd panoply of Washing-day,
Zephyrs the flutt'ring crowd inspire, uplift,
Distend the shirt, and agitate the shift;
But should perchance th' afflatus breathe too strong,
The treach'rous prop precipitates the throng:
Let such sublime disaster oft attend your song.
"Ever you'll find me, your complaisant Muse,

219

Quick to inspire, whate'er the theme you choose –
Dunghills, or feather-beds, or fat-tail'd rams,
Or rum, or kilts, or eggs, or bugs, or yams.
So when some dame, in some Department Store,
Her shopping-list exhausted, orders more,
The sleek assistant, outwardly unvex'd,
Smiling exclaims, 'Thanks, moddom! And the next'
"Behold the pompous funerary train
Of Enoch Arden, piscatorial swain.
'Mid tropic seas the luckless Bryan mark,
In process of bisection by a shark.
Hear ARMSTRONG gloat on what occurs inside you
When cook has turtle-soup'd and ven'son-pie'd you;
And list while DYER, in Miltonic metre,
Recites the ailments of the fleecy bleater.
Rejoice with YOUNG that no protective bars
Exclude commercial blessings from the stars,
And in the Milky Way prepare to greet
A still more glorious Throgmorton Street.
Hear DARWIN, whom no scand'lous detail ruffles,
Record the love-lorn loneliness of truffles,
Frisking of vegetable lads and lasses,
Amours of oysters, goings-on of gases.
With fit solemnity let WORDSWORTH tell
How Simon's ankles swell, and swell, and swell,
And how, from Anna's couch when friends depart,
An owl, preserv'd by taxidermic art,
Can cheat the tedious time, and heal the conscious smart
"So sing the Masters of Bathetic Verse.

Follow their lead: do better, doing worse.
So shall your brows be crown'd with bays unwith'ring;
So shall the world be blither for your blith'ring;
So–"
Here she pauses, deep inhales the breeze,
And shakes the earth with cataclysmic sneeze,
The dust-heaps crumble, whirling clouds arise,
And all is blotted from my blinking eyes.

This "proem" was written as an introduction to an anthology of bad verse entitled The Stuffed Owl, which was collected and edited by Charles Lee and D B Wyndham Lewis, with cartoons by Max Beerbohm. It was published by Dent in 1930.

BIBLIOGRAPHY

THE WIDOW WOMAN

Serialised in The Leisure Hour 1896

THE WIDOW WOMAN

First Edition James Bowden 1897

THE WIDOW WOMAN

Second Edition James Bowden 1899

THE WIDOW WOMAN

Third Edition Gibbings (London) J A D Bridger (Penzance) 1907

THE WIDOW WOMAN

Fourth Edition J M Dent Illustrated by Charles E Brock 1911

THE WIDOW WOMAN

Fifth Edition J M Dent Illustrated by Charles E Brock 1912

THE WIDOW WOMAN

Fifth Edition reprint J M Dent The Wayfarer's Library Illustrated by Charles E Brock (undated)

PAUL CARAH CORNISHMAN

James Bowden Illustrated by Gordon Browne 1898 (Dent reprint 1911)

CYNTHIA IN THE WEST

Grant Richards 1900

OUR LITTLE TOWN
AND OTHER CORNISH TALES AND FANCIES

Gibbings 1909

Includes Our Little Town (Penticost's, A Question of Taste, The Defeat of the Amazons, The Silk Hat, A Government Alliance, Ned's House, Fanny and Cornelius), Mr Sampson, The White Bonnet, A Strong Man, The

Lucubrations of Thyrza Theophila (A Primitive Pot, Further Communications [reprinted from The Leisure Hour by permission of The Religious Tract Society]), Langarrock Great Tree, Wisht Wood, St Lidgy and the Giant, Tram Trist

OUR LITTLE TOWN

AND OTHER CORNISH TALES AND FANCIES

J M Dent (and E P Dutton, New York) 1911

Includes Our Little Town (Penticost's, A Question of Taste, The Defeat of the Amazons, The Silk Hat, A Government Alliance, Ned's House, Fanny and Cornelius), Mr Sampson, The White Bonnet, A Strong Man, The Lucubrations of Thyrza Theophila (A Primitive Pot, Further Communications), Langarrock Great Tree, Wisht Wood, St Lidgy and the Giant, Tram Trist

OUR LITTLE TOWN

J M Dent The Wayfarer's Library 1928

Includes Our Little Town (Penticost's, A Question of Taste, The Defeat of the Amazons, The Silk Hat, A Government Alliance, Ned's House, Fanny and Cornelius), Mr Sampson and Pascoe's Song (for the first time). Cover features a photograph of Ernest Selley dressed in the costume of Mr Sampson for a performance of the Welwyn (sic) Garden City Players

DORINDA'S BIRTHDAY

J M Dent Illustrated by Herbert Cole 1911

MR SAMPSON (A PLAY)

J M Dent 1912

This play was awarded the Lord Howard de Walden Cup in the British Drama League's Festival of Community Drama in 1926, and the David Belasco Cup in the New York Little Theatre Tournament in 1927. It was first performed by Letchworth Dramatic Society in 1911

THE BANNS OF MARRIAGE (A PLAY)

J M Dent 1927

A QUESTION OF TASTE

J M Dent Aldine Chapbook Illustrated by Roberta Waudby 1930

VALE OF LANHERNE

Dyllansow Truran 1984 Edited by Phyl Hellyar

WEST COUNTRY SHORT STORIES

Faber 1949

Chosen by Lewis Wilshire – contains Mr Sampson

CORNISH TALES

J M Dent 1941 (and 1946)

The Widow Woman, Our Little Town, Dorinda's Birthday, Mr Sampson, Pascoe's Song, The White Bonnet

TWENTY ONE-ACT PLAYS

Dent and Dutton 1938

Selected by John Hampden – contains Mr Sampson

ONE AND ALL

London Museum Press 1951

Edited by Denys Val Baker – includes The Defeat Of The Amazons (from Our Little Town)

THE STUFFED OWL

J M Dent 1930

An Anthology of Bad Verse selected and arranged by D B Wyndham Lewis and Charles Lee, with an introductory 'Proem' by Charles Lee and cartoons by Max Beerbohm

CORNISH MAGAZINE

Joseph Pollard July 1898-May 1899

Edited by Sir Arthur Quiller Couch – includes Wisht Wood, A Strong Man, Penticost's, A Question of Taste, The Defeat of the Amazons, St Lidgy and the Giant

CORNISH SHORT STORIES

Penguin 1976

Edited by Denys Val Baker – includes The Defeat of the Amazons

MODERN PLAYS IN ONE ACT

Edited by A Mordaunt Sharp – contains Mr Sampson 1928

FURTHER READING

THE CORNISH JOURNAL OF CHARLES LEE
Tabb House 1995
Edited by K C Phillipps

THE CORNISH REVIEW
Charles Lee by H J Willmott Summer 1949

AN BANER KERNEWEK
A Foreigner in Pendennack by Derek Williams (Number 62) 1990

NEWLYN OF YESTERDAY
Ben Batten 1983

JOURNAL OF THE ROYAL INSTITUTION OF CORNWALL
Charles Lee and the Cornish Dialect by Ken Phillipps 1989

OLD CORNWALL
Charles Lee at St Mawgan-in-Pydar and Pascoe's Song by H M Cresswell
Payne Volume V, No 8 1957

BROADCASTS AND PRODUCTIONS

PANTOMIMES
Charles Lee wrote a number of satirical pantomimes for Letchworth
Garden City. They were performed at Cloisters, a theatre run by a Miss
Lawrence, and at The Skittles, a dry pub

THE WIDOW WOMAN
A stage adaptation by Violet Bluett performed at several venues in
Cornwall, including Truro and Coverack, by the Truro Play Actors during
the 1950s. The cast included Gwendoline Carmichael as Mrs Elizabeth
Pollard and Violet Bluett as Mary Poljew, WJ Tucker as John Trelill,
Margery Tonkin as Vassie Jenkin, Harold Tonkin as Clunker, Joan Tonkin
as Nanny, Dorothy Ashton as Lucy Jane, Fernleigh Bluett as Cap'n Billy
Jenkin, Daisy Delbridge as Mrs Pezzack, Frank Jewell as 'Siah Pezzack

The Widow Woman

A radio play by Becky Hocking, produced by Owen Reed, first broadcast on the West of England Home Service 10th March 1948

Mr Sampson

Adapted for broadcast by A G Brooks, first broadcast on the West of England Home Service 1st April 1953

Pascoe's Song

Adapted for broadcast by Aileen Mills, first broadcast on the West of England Home Service 9th November 1955

Mr Sampson

First performed at Letchworth in November 1910 – it won a number of awards, was performed by numerous amateur dramatic societies, and recorded for BBC radio and television, both in Britain and abroad

Our Little Town

A series of six 30-minute film adaptations recorded in 1979 and broadcast in 1980 by HTV Wales and HTV West. They were adapted by Denis Constanduros, directed by Terry Harding, produced by Leonard White, edited by Stuart Edwards, with music composed by Sydney Sager and performed by Jack Emblow and Michael Copley. It was designed by Ken Jones and the executive producer was Patrick Dromgoole. The series was entitled Our Little Town and the episodes included The Joker (The White Bonnet), Mr Sampson, The Stranger's Gift (The Silk Hat), The Great Harmonium Contest (Fanny and Cornelius), The Amazons (Defeat of the Amazons). Among the actors taking part were Rowena Cooper, Tim Preece, John Malcolm, Daphne Heard, Ivor Salter, Paul Nicholson, Linsey Hayes and Mike Hope. It is clear that the series was made on a shoestring, with cheap and unrealistic sets. What is most disappointing is that none of Lee's language is retained and there is no use of authentic dialect. The only clue to the fact that the stories originated in Cornwall is the use of a sepia panoramic view of old Mousehole under the credits

Our Little Town

Theatre production devised by Pauline Sheppard, toured briefly in the autumn of 1997 to St Ives, Penzance, Phillack, Paul, St Just, Zennor and

Newlyn, and as a shortened piece for four voices in 1998 at Wadebridge Folk Festival. It was presented as a play for voices with a few hand props. The cast included David Shaw, Pauline Sheppard, Grevis Williams, Rik Williams, Dawn Barnes, Dave Trahair, Julia Twomlow, Stephen Hall, Stephanie Hayward and Anna Murphy, with original music by John Bickersteth, Neil McPhail and Nick McLeod

SHOWS FOR THE NEWYLN SCHOOL OF PAINTERS

Musical shows written by Lee, the proceeds from which were donated to the Newlyn Artists Dramatic Society plus other charities. Those taking part included Edwin Harris, Thomas Cooper Gotch, John da Costa, Henry Rheam, John Crooke, Frederick Evans, Percy Craft, Walter Langley, Samuel Green Enderby, W H A Theed, AR Davies, Charles Trevor Garland, Ernest Robert Ireland Blackburne, Lionel Birch and Fred Hall, with Lee credited as the musical director and composer. There is a surviving poster for one of these concerts, which reads: "On no account attend the Dark Seance to be held at St John's Hall, Penzance on March 5th and 6th 1894 at 8pm by that unique little lot of Unartistic Incapable Aboriginal Amateurs known to the police as Lubly Lobengula's Impecunious Impi. Greatest efforts will be made to provide a dull and uninteresting programme. All vocal and instrumental music strictly out of time and tune. Horrible tortures will be inflicted on the audience."

REVIEWS

Every lover of good humour, good observation and good writing will read this with pleasure
— DAILY TELEGRAPH

Pre-eminently and unquestionably the very voice of the delectable Duchy – they should be owned by all who relish the simple and eternal in human nature
— THE OBSERVER

Life as represented in these stories will be, to persons not acquainted with Cornwall and its people, the revelation of a new world
— THE TIMES

Clever, humourous and thoroughly enjoyable
— THE SCOTSMAN

Cornwall did something for Charles Lee that it has done for many another sensitive writer and artist: it liberated his spirit in these tales which are so near to perfection
— H J WILLMOTT, CORNISH GUARDIAN

Never have I found such a feast of interest. These short stories are first rate
— DAILY MAIL

Gentle and scholarly humour, and the nicest precision in portraiture
— SUNDAY TIMES

Lee's technique was masterly, and he had an exceptionally

lively mind. As we say in Cornwall 'he don't miss much'

— KEN PHILLIPPS

There is hardly a thing that one would question in his usage of dialect

— A L ROWSE

There are sentences one longs to quote and scenes one would like to transcribe to show the delightfulness and merit of the work. Get the book, and spend two hours in the inmost life of a Cornish fishing village, and come away refreshed, even as though its clean salt breezes had been blowing in your face and filling your mind with healthy, charming ideas about even the ugly things of life

— THE GRAPHIC

Irresistible humour

— ILLUSTRATED LONDON NEWS

A vein of quiet, dry humour

— NEW YORK EVENING POST

As brisk and exhilarating as a draught of cider

— THE ACADEMY

Possessing not merely period charm, but qualities of wit, honesty and truth

— BEN BATTEN

Mr Lee gives us an exquisitely perfect picture of a Cornish fishing village

— THE OUTLOOK

As refreshing as a breeze from the Atlantic. Vivid, homely, fresh, natural and picturesque – it is the book to take up at the end of a fagging day

— CHRISTIAN WORLD

There is nothing in Lee's dialect to estrange the English reader; the stories should never have been allowed to fall into oblivion. The sketches and short stories show the now rare conviction that the way to reveal character is through narrative, not analysis

— TIMES LITERARY SUPPLEMENT

I have always thought, and still do, that the language in the Widow Woman is the nearest a writer has got to recapturing the Newlyn 'chat'

— DOUGLAS WILLIAMS

The picturesqueness of a remote land where manners and customs and speech and the philosophy of life have not yet lost their individuality under the levelling roller of our uniform modern civilisation

— NEW YORK DAILY TRIBUNE

Extraordinarily human

— THE ATHENAEUM

As a background to this picture of eager life with its underlying pathos we have the sparkling lines of the Cornish coast drawn lovingly by a master hand. From first to last, a book of unusual charm

— WESTMINSTER GAZETTE

Thoroughly realised and admirably presented

— SATURDAY REVIEW

I remember the delight, faintly tinged with envy, with which I first read Charles Lee. I can now offer him, for what it's worth, a Cornishman's tribute of regard, with a fellow writer's assurance that all good writing has a mysterious way of arriving. As a piece of writing, in prose clear and tunable, I had to admire every page. And there are also flashes of genuinely poetical imagination

— SIR ARTHUR QUILLER-COUCH

NOTES ON THE COLLECTION

ONE MAY Day in the early 1980s I went to a London bookfair and came across a row of books relating to Cornwall, including Randigal Rhymes and a Glossary of Cornish Words by Joseph Thomas, 1895.

My late husband, Ken, was not only a Cornishman but also an academic, one of whose great interests was the historical relationship between dialect and Standard English. Consequently we always bought dialect glossaries whenever possible, especially those of the 19th century. I took down the book and on the end paper was pencilled 'Charles Lee 1895'.

Now Charles Lee I had heard of – in fact some years earlier we had made a pilgrimage to Mawgan to meet an octogenarian who had known Lee.

Ken had long been an admirer of Lee's depiction of Cornish provincial life, and of his keen ear for the nuances of dialect; and the Thomas' Glossary I had just picked up was a veritable treasure-trove for a language scholar, crammed as it was with Lee's erudite annotations in tiny, neat handwriting.

There were parallels cited from the whole gamut of English Literature (Chaucer, Malory, Spenser, Shakespeare, Southey, Hardy etc.) and from America (Twain, Lowell); and Lee noted cognates in the Italian of Boccaccio and the

French of Rabelais, in Gaelic, Breton, Welsh and Friesian, in Old Norse, Old English, Old Cornish and others.

Most writers on Cornish dialect have tended to see its survival as an entertaining curiosity, but Lee treated it with scholarly analysis and respect.

I bought the book and then I looked at the others on the shelf. They were mostly novels about Cornwall and all had Lee's signature in them.

Curious to know where this cache of books had come from I asked the bookseller. He was from Letchworth and had bought the books locally from someone with connections with Lee. He couldn't give me the vendor's name without permission, but he agreed to contact him and to pass on our telephone number.

We didn't really expect to hear anything more, but we did, and one Saturday afternoon Ken and I drove to Letchworth and met Mr and Mrs G Jones, who had inherited Lee's house and effects.

We bought Lee's notes on things Cornish, including the five notebooks that form a commentary on his time in Cornwall between 1892 and 1908. They were put aside to await Ken's retirement. Finally, in 1995 his edited version, The Cornish Journal of Charles Lee, was published by Tabb House of Padstow.

– Pat Phillipps
Mount 2001